PHELIM McG(

G000130973

He's F----

REFLECTIONS ON THE RISEN CHRIST
AND THE COMING OF THE HOLY SPIRIT

To Anne & Paddy

With much love & gratitude

for all your friendship, support &

love over the years,

Phelim.

THE COLUMBA PRESS
DUBLIN 2001

THE COLUMBA PRESS
55A Spruce Avenue, Stillorgan Industrial Park,
Blackrock, Co Dublin

First edition 2001
Cover by Bill Bolger
Reproduction of *The Resurrection* by Bonifazio de Pitati,
courtesy of The National Gallery of Ireland.
Origination by
The Columba Press
Printed in Ireland by
Colour Books Ltd, Dublin

ISBN 1 85607 330 0

Acknowledgements
I express my gratitude to all who have made the publication of
this book possible, especially the parishioners of the Sacred
Heart Parish, Wimbledon. In particular I wish to record my
thanks to Hugh Johnston for his untiring work on the com-
puter, to Louise Taylor for the many hours she spent on the
script and to Mary Hayes for her professional proof-reading,
without whose help this book would never have seen the light
of day. I am indebted to the following authors for the inspiration
I gained from their writings: R. Brown, W. Barclay, E. Farrell,
A. Padovano, D. McBride, D. Stanley, A. Tilby, and many others.
Above all, I am grateful to my fellow Jesuits, Frs J. Hyde and
P. Kennedy, for their deep spirituality and the influence it had
on me.

Phelim McGowan SJ

Contents

Foreword

There are many good books to help us ponder and pray the great seasons of Advent and Lent. Yet there are few to help us enter the beautiful season of Eastertide. It almost seems as if, in practice, devotion to Jesus and, through him, to his Father, stops at his death. Maybe, like his friends, we are emotionally exhausted and cannot grasp the awe-filled and joyful events that were to follow.

Lent deals with the momentous events of Jesus' passion and death on the cross. The Christian can identify with all this to a certain extent, but what of Jesus' resurrection and risen life as experienced by those first disciples? Could the Christian enter into and share Jesus' joy? Newman, in one of his sermons for Easter, makes the point, 'At Christmas we joy with the natural unmixed joy of children, but at Easter our joy is highly wrought and refined in character.' This part of Jesus' life is elusive and the Christian is not totally at ease with it. Part of the reason is that Jesus' presence has changed and is totally new. The whole atmosphere, both physical and relational, is different from those meetings he had with his friends and people in general. Now it is calmer, usually taking place in the early morning or late at night, in a quiet place. Here the risen Christ comes as Consoler to his grief-stricken friends, bringing them back to life so that he can send them out on a mission with the good news that death has been overcome and that he is risen. It is a call to faith, faith that the aim and goal of life is to be joyful with the risen Jesus before his Father. Therefore, the Easter experiences must be read, pondered and prayed in a different manner from the events of Jesus' mortal life if we are to experience the joy to which Newman refers. The aim of *He is Risen* is to help the Christian savour that joy.

Phelim McGowan SJ
Sacred Heart Church
Wimbledon, London
8 September 2000, Birthday of Our Lady

CHAPTER ONE

Easter Silence

There is a strange, somewhat awesome silence between Jesus' death on Good Friday and his resurrection on Easter Sunday, so what do we do with Holy Saturday? We face a confusing nothingness between the Good Friday liturgy and the Holy Saturday night vigil, so how do we cope with it? How do we cope with a day that seems so empty; a void that offers no hint of life or hope? It is the only day in the whole of the church's year when there is no liturgy, and yet we feel an instinctive impulse to 'do' something.

It is much the same experience we have when anyone very close to us dies – we find ourselves at a loss about what to do from the time of the actual death until the burial. It is the most difficult time, because it is the in-between time. Somebody has gone and no one can take his place. We need time to absorb what has happened, to adjust. Shrouded in loss we don't know what to do. There is little anyone can do. A strange silence descends.

This is the silence that we experience on Holy

Saturday. It is not like any other silence; it is a silence proper only to the state of 'being dead'. There is a sense of awe, a realisation that something tremendous has happened. This is the silence that enfolds the dead Jesus on the cross and in the tomb. Holy Saturday silence is, at the same time, both the silence and the feast of the 'dead God'. Silence in this context is not the same as 'not talking', for there is more to it than the mere absence of words. A lot is happening. In the presence and moment of death, communication takes place without words, because no words can express the emotions experienced by those left behind.

It is difficult to share the silence of loss – it is not that words are not useful at such moments, but rather, that in such moments no words are adequate to express the sense of loss, and so it's only silence that seems appropriate. Perhaps the only way we can pray at such a time is by expressing helplessness in silence before the Lord.

It is said that 'birth is the beginning of death, but death is the beginning of life'. In one sense this sums up what is happening during the silence of Holy Saturday. When a human being is conceived, and in the first weeks that follow, there is little or no perceptible activity, and yet we know that the greatest of events is taking place; life itself is being created (Ps 139:13-15). In the darkness of the womb, the child is satisfied with what it has because it is ignorant of the world outside until the moment comes when it is painfully thrust into the light (Jn 1:5) and welcomed by those who are ready to love it. A community of love awaits it. Yet, from the moment we are conceived we are preparing for another birth; sooner or later, we will suffer the birth pangs that thrust us into the presence of God, our Father (Jn 19:30b). God the Father, Prodigal of Love, awaits the moment of rebirth when he will welcome his child home, 'Well done, my good and faithful servant, enter into the joy of the Lord' (Mt 25:34). Silent prayer is perhaps the only way of rehearsing that moment, a way of entering into the atmosphere of two people in love being reunited. It is a welcoming home. The Holy Spirit will effect this quality of presence in us, because it is she who brings the Father and Jesus together in awesome silence.

The silence of Holy Saturday will eventually merge into the silence of Easter Week. This experience of Easter silence will deepen as we reflect on how the risen Jesus brings the gift of life to his friends during his many appearances to them. It is no mere accident that Jesus chooses to appear to his friends at times and in places when nature itself is stilled and peaceful; he doesn't 'break through' or 'shatter' the silence with a great burst of noise; rather, he enters into it and through it shares its strength with those he loves. This silence is almost tangible when Jesus appears apparently from nowhere; 'at dawn' (Mt 28:1), 'while it was still dark', 'on the evening of the same day' (Jn 20:19), 'in the garden' (Jn 20:11), 'in a locked room', 'on the quiet country road on the Sabbath' (Lk 24:13), 'by the lakeside in the early morning before breakfast' (Jn 21:1), 'on the mountain' (Mt 29:16). It is not that Jesus refuses to meet his friends in the Temple or in Jerusalem but, to begin with, they need this silence in order to grasp what has really happened to their friend and Lord. It is essential that they have this time away from the noise and bustle of the temple (Jn 2:13-14), or the busy streets (Mk 5:31), where his voice was often drowned by the noise of the crowd. They are trying to come to terms with his absence, an absence which, at first, they can perceive only as something negative. We need this silence too, if he is to come to us. 'Father, if you do not speak, fill my heart with your silence' is a good prayer for Holy Saturday and Eastertide. This is a time when we need the divine silence which comes from God the Father (Wis 19:14-15).

We need this silence in order to hear the voice of Jesus, and also that of his Father in the voice of other people. The word 'person' comes from the Latin root 'per-sonare', to sound through, and throughout the gospels, Jesus, whose listening is total, shows us what this means in practice. For example, the woman who was to be stoned to death for adultery says only a few words: 'No one, Sir' (Jn 8:11) and yet Jesus is also listening to what she is not saying; he listens simultaneously to the words and the person since the two are one. The actual words she utters are less important than what her whole being is expressing. Jesus is aware of her own unique giftedness and personality (Mt 10:20). By listening to the whole of her, by resisting the temptation to listen only to what she's saying and to settle for see-ing her only as an interesting character, by not allowing himself to be distracted by her special qual-ities, by focusing totally on her, Jesus helps her to recognise her own giftedness. He listens respectfully to the one who is speaking to him, and sees before him a daughter loved by his Father. He can only do this because he is already filled with divine silence. This enables Jesus not to be distracted by the present circumstances, her reputation or prejudice. Imbued with divine silence, Jesus can look beyond the present and see the woman's true self, the person she could be.

John's gospel is filled with such examples; e.g. the Samaritan Woman (Jn 4:19-40), the Blind Man (Jn 9:7, 38-39), the Demoniac who was cured (Mk. 5:19-20) and many others. Having enabled these people to reveal their real selves, the people God created them to be. Jesus goes further and helps them to become aware of the love and truth they, in their turn, reveal to him and to others. For the apostles and for us to do the same we, too, need divine silence, and the only way to acquire it is to pray to the Holy Spirit:

'If you do not speak, fill my heart with your silence.'

CHAPTER TWO

Easter and Watching

There is another reason for Easter silence. Mary of Magdala and the women were waiting for the dawn that would end the Sabbath so that they could come and anoint their friend, Jesus (Mk 16:1-2). They are forced to wait before they can tend his body. Meanwhile, there is nothing they can do and they wait in silence. Silence usually accompanies waiting and watching, which is often a negative experience. We become impatient. We keep glancing at our watch, looking constantly in the direction from which we expect the train or bus to arrive. Perhaps we walk up and down in silence, or utter a few expressions of anger or irritation. Stuck in a stationary train just outside the station, we feel frustrated and may be tempted to get out and walk the short distance to the platform, regardless of the danger. The frustration grows because we feel we have no control over what's happening. It is a sign of our helplessness when we want to shout 'Don't just sit there ... do something!' It all appears such a waste of time.

Yet, waiting and looking can be a very positive experience; for example, waiting to meet your best friend whom you have not seen for ages. Being a close friend, he or she is on your mind. As you become more aware of your friend, your thoughts start to preoccupy you. You become excited anticipating his arrival. The very act of waiting colours the whole of your day; he may be late or early; may be wearing clothing you don't immediately recognise etc. Aware of this you will be more attentive, searching for your friend, you will notice keenly all that is going on around you. While you are waiting you cannot really 'settle' down to do anything. You are aware of all that interferes with the anticipation of the arrival; you do not really pay attention to the weather, to your hunger or to anything that happens around you, or in you (Jn 20:11). You do not speak because you do not know what to say ... you're just simply 'waiting'. You are too caught up in expectation. It has all been worthwhile; the more the heart longs to see and welcome your friend, the greater the love and welcome your friend will receive when he or she arrives (Jn 20:17). The present can only really begin again once he or she comes.

This waiting can be a good entrance into prayer, as Jesus himself tells us (Mt 24:44, 25:13). In fact, in

1 Tim 5:2, Paul describes Jesus' coming as 'like a thief in the night'. Maybe this is what happens to Mary of Magdala and the other women in Mk 16:1ff. Their only reported words are: 'Who will roll away the stone for us from the entrance to the tomb?' Yet, by being there, waiting and looking, they are rewarded with the gift of the good news of Jesus' resurrection. It is by being quietly present and open to the awesome, earth-shattering news that 'He is risen' enters their hearts and terrifies them 'out of their wits'. This is their first reaction to the resurrection of Jesus (Mt 28:5, Lk 24:37).

The women run off telling no one because they are afraid. Their fear is understandable because of what had happened to the apostles and to them a couple of days before Jesus' capture in Gethsemane, his trial and suffering, his being whipped and crowned with thorns, his walking the Way of the Cross, enduring a criminal's death by crucifixion, and finally his burial (Mk 16:6, Mt 28:5). They are simply overwhelmed. They desperately need to hear Jesus' greeting, 'Do-not-be-afraid ...' (Mt 28:10), but they also need silence and attentiveness to be able to hear it.

This first reaction is important for us as we try to appreciate the power of the resurrection and its meaning. If we are not terrified as they were, then perhaps we are missing its real meaning. We might be tempted on hearing the good news to be astonished, but then, filled with joy, go on to tell everybody we meet that 'Jesus has conquered death and is risen'. Then everybody would rejoice, but it would not be enough. This is why we need the Holy Spirit: firstly, to help us meditate on the events of Jesus' death and the resurrection but then to help us become immersed in the atmosphere of Easter (Lk 24:11). When Jesus actually appears in their midst, they are (verse 35) 'in a state of alarm and fright'. Initially, as a result of waiting and looking, they feel alarm and fright, fear and doubt although they had joyfully exchanged the good news. Jesus, who throughout his 'public' life as a preacher, who waited on his friends to understand his good news (Jn 14:9), is willing to wait once again for their return to him. When they do return, they are rewarded with the words 'Do not be afraid' (Jn 28:10). That is the beginning of their understanding of the resurrection, and it is ours as well. It is could also be our prayer.

CHAPTER THREE

Appearances of Jesus

(Song 3:1-2): We need to watch and wait because Jesus appears and disappears suddenly and without explanation. It was obviously quite frightening for the disciples, hence Jesus' words of reassurance: 'Peace be with you' (Jn 20:19). The evangelists never elaborate on these comings and goings, because they do not know or understand any more than we do. On only one occasion is there a description of Jesus' disappearance. It is in the account of the Emmaus scene when the writer records: 'He vanished from their sight.' Realising this, we should ask the Holy Spirit to help us understand: 'Lord, let me know your ways; Lord, teach me your paths.'

The risen Jesus is different insofar as he does not seem to be the Jesus of Nazareth the disciples had known before his death. In fact, there is an atmosphere of unreality about him, an unreality that renders him a total stranger to them. Even when the disciples do know who he is, when he appears on the Tiberias shore, they hesitate to speak his name (Jn 21:12). Somehow he has changed. The old familiar feeling

of companionship associated with knowing and
being known by Jesus of Nazareth, the ordinary
man of flesh and blood, has gone and, in its place,
he is a man whose heart is filled with a deep sense of
peace, trust and belief. Why this change? Perhaps it
is due to the terrific joy that swept over his Father's
face as he raised his Son to eternal life. 'Well done,
my good and faithful servant, enter into the joy of
the Lord. Because you have been faithful over small
things, I will place you over great. Come and join in
your Master's happiness' (Mt 25:21). Was it the over-
whelming joy, with which the Father greeted Jesus
that changed the old familiar Jesus of earth into the
Christ of heaven? In his joy, a joy fully charged with
the Holy Spirit, Jesus says: 'Abba, Father'. Jesus'
prayer has reached its climax; he can enter into the
heart of the psalmist's joy: 'I rejoiced when I heard
them say, Let us go to God's house' (Ps 11:22). These
words are fulfilled as Jesus returns home. The goal
of Jesus' life is to be 'at home' with the Father (Jn
17:24) and it is ours, too. As Jesus prayed (Ps 122) to
his Father through the Holy Spirit, so too, the Spirit
can give us the power to hear Jesus praying, not only
for his friends, but for each of us individually.

The change in Jesus could also be due to the fact
that love is only complete when everything is shared
with those you love. Jesus now wants to share his

divinity with his relatives and friends, to show them who he really is: the Son of God (Jn 15:15). Given their religious belief of God being One (Deut 6:4-5), Jesus had to meet them frequently over a period of time in order to help them assimilate this amazing truth. Perhaps this is why he appeared only to his devoted followers. He was able to create in them a Christian faith, because their love for him opened them up to receive such an unexpected favour. He could have appeared to Annas, Caiaphas, Pilate etc., but his purpose was not merely to persuade people that he was alive again. His purpose was to allow them to see that he had entered into a completely different existence with his Father. Because they really knew Jesus, the disciples were able to understand his actions and his teachings. They realised the significance not only of what was said and done, but also what was left unsaid and undone. Jesus needed them to have this understanding so they could be his interpreters to the world. He was divine and he turned the world upside down! Through Jesus, God was finally revealed as a God who is Father, someone who is completely self-effacing, a loving father who will go after the 'lost' sheep, the depressed and the lonely. This Christian knowledge is not a purely verbal message that can be relayed to others; it is the experience of a divine relationship, a message which is intended not only to change peoples' ideas but radically to alter their lives (Lk 24:32). It is not just a story about a man. It is an unimaginable phenomenon. The God-made-man has become alive again in a different way (Jn 11:25). That is why the Holy Spirit has to 'remind' the disciples of all that Jesus had said to them (Jn 11:26) and this is also why his Father sends the Holy Spirit on us (Jn 14:26).

Somehow this new life, this new existence with his Father, does not separate Jesus from his mortal body. Jesus is still able to eat with his friends (Lk 24:42-43), Thomas is able to touch his wounds (Jn 20:27), Mary can hear him speak her name (Jn 20:16). It is clear that he is still the old Jesus. The resurrection of Jesus shows that all the relationships he's had during his lifetime, all the emotions, experiences, events, growths, joys, sorrows, disappointments and so forth have made him the person he is and always will be.

The risen Jesus has chosen to remain human forever (Lk 2:52). In this way he teaches his friends, and each one of us who have lived thereafter, that our vocation is to be truly ourselves, to be thoroughly human, to believe, despite external appearances. We may and indeed must hope to enjoy God even within the corporeal and material side of our personalities. The more human we become, the more true to ourselves and the more Christ-like we become. Jesus lived on earth in order to teach us how to become completely human (Mt 5:44-48). Jesus came to redeem the whole person, not merely to 'save our souls'. We always need to thank God our Father for creating us human beings (Ps 139:13-14), and to thank Jesus for overcoming our refusals of love and reintroducing us to his Father (Lk 23:34). Paradoxically, the more we, his followers, are drawn into Jesus' humanity, the greater the faith, hope and love we will need because now we need to have Christian faith, Christian hope and Christian love (Jn 20:29).

Our inherent human gifts of believing, hoping and loving will be deepened. Because Jesus himself believed, hoped and loved, he was able to assist his friends, the disciples, and us, his friends and disciples of today, in recognising these gifts and gradually become permeated by them. How rarely, if ever, do we thank him for these gifts.

Very often, a person is only fully appreciated after his or her death. The full meaning of the scriptures, which Jesus announced during his earthly ministry, was that he would become a living and dynamic force for all, but only after he was delivered up to death. Jesus' humanity, his believing, hoping, loving and dying, sum up everything that united to make him what he is. In his own words: 'I am the Resurrection and the Life' (Jn 11:25).

CHAPTER FOUR

The Holy Spirit and Presence

How Jesus appears and disappears during the post-resurrection period is not explained. He seems elusive, coming and going, and not as available as he was before. Something new has happened. His presence is somehow different, perhaps deeper than before, and maybe this is why the prayer of Easter requires a deeper faith. The prayer suggested is that of the father of the epileptic boy, 'I do have faith; help the little faith that I have' (Mk 9:24).

During his public ministry, Jesus gave his friends signs and wonders and asked them to believe in them even if they could not believe him (Jn 10:38). The time after Easter is not the time for miracles but for a deeper faith in him. It is time for a faith permeated not just by the Holy Spirit but by the Spirit of the risen Christ, that is the Spirit of God man. We need to pray to God our Father to give us this Spirit. As Jesus says, 'If you then, who are evil, know how to give your children what is good, how much more will our heavenly Father give the Holy Spirit to those who ask him' (Lk 9:13).

It is only towards the end of his life that Jesus speaks of the Holy Spirit (Jn 15:26, 16:7-15). It is only in the context of leaving his friends, for example, when he needs them to be his witnesses, to enlighten people about sin, and about who was in the right, and about judgement, that he speaks of sending his Spirit. It is only therefore in the context of his departure or absence that his friends understand why he will send his Spirit. It is when they feel they will no longer have his support, when they are filled with sadness (Jn 16:6-7), that he promises to send the Spirit of consolation. It is to their advantage that he goes; unless he does the Holy Spirit cannot come to them.

They would not have been totally unfamiliar with this idea. They knew the incident in the Old Testament where Elijah passed on his spirit to Elisha, his servant, in answer to Elisha's petition (2 Kings 2:9-15). Throughout the Old Testament, God the Father sent his Spirit to the prophets (Ezek 2:2), to Simeon, (1 Kings 2: 25) and finally to Mary (Lk 1:35). Jesus explained to his friends and anybody willing to listen to him, the mind and ways of his Father, but his explanation was limited (Jn 14:9). It needed a deeper sending of his Spirit (Jn 20:22), to help them assimilate all that he had said and done (Jn

14:26). Without the help of the Spirit of God made man, they would be unable to preach the good news to a disbelieving world (2 Cor 5:18-20). Without the help of his Spirit, they would not have been able to pray (Rom 8:26-27) in the way he had taught them (Mt 14:23, Lk 6:12). Above all, they needed this Spirit of God made man to help them understand who Jesus really was. Mary, for example, realised he was the Messiah because of her annunciation experience but she had not grasped that he was also divine. This needed a deeper sending (Jn 7:39); and it was the same for his friends. It was through his appearances and disappearances after his death that he taught them he was divine. Jesus' friends missed him because they had been very close to him. He, therefore, remained alive for them in their minds and in their hearts (Lk 24:19-24, 33-35, Jn 20:8-9). In this way he was able to be with them again (Rom 8:38-39). In scripture, his presences and absences are found from beginning to end. It remains the constant paradox:

Jer 31:3: 'Yahweh had appeared to him from afar; I have loved you with an everlasting love, So I am constant in my affection for you'.

Deut 31:17: 'On that day my anger shall blaze against them; I will forsake them and hide my face from them'.

Jesus also experiences both the presence then the absence of the Holy Spirit. 'Listen, the time will come, in fact it has come already, when you will be scattered, each going his own way and leaving me alone. And yet I am not alone, because the Father is with me' (Jn 16:32). See also ' My God, my God, why have you deserted me?' (Mk 15:34b) Because our human minds cannot adequately handle both these aspects of God at the same time, we have to emphasise one aspect or the other. Our relationship with God is one of presence and absence. Both occur continuously and simultaneously, throughout our earthly lives. The risen Jesus, by his appearances ('presences') and disappearances ('absences') gives a human expression to this divine presence. Jesus wants Mary of Magdala not to cling onto his physical presence but to find his spirit, the Spirit of God made man, amongst his friends (Jn 20:17). In his absence paradoxically she will find his presence (Mt 18:20). His friends, like Mary of Magdala can only talk about the Jesus they know (Jn 20:25). In any human friendship, the more that friends know of one another, the more they realise there are parts they hide from one another, parts that may be glimpsed from time to time. Jesus uses this everyday human experience to explain his divinity, that gift he now wishes to share with his chosen ones. In our cele-

bration of the eucharist, we reach the depths of the
sacramental presence (Lk 22:19-20) yet we are told to
'go in peace to love and serve the Lord'. God can
somehow be both absent and present at the same
time and it is in these absences and presences of
Jesus that he shows that he is God. As Jesus himself
said, it is only through the Holy Spirit that we, like
his friends, will be able to grasp his friendship. Only
she can help us to understand God's ways, as so
clearly expressed in Is 55:8-9:

> 'For my thoughts are not your thoughts,
> my ways not your ways – it is Yahweh who speaks.
> Yes, the heavens are as high above earth
> As my ways are above your ways,
> My thoughts above your thoughts.'

CHAPTER FIVE

Easter Faith

Some of Jesus' friends waited and watched on Calvary and witnessed his death (Jn 19:25). They continued to do so when they could in the burial garden after the Sabbath (Jn 19:41-42). Yet, there was no one there to witness his resurrection. Nobody saw it nor could have seen it for it is beyond human understanding (1 Cor 15:35-38), because it is not like the resuscitation of a dead body like the daughter of Jairus (Lk 8:49-53), nor Lazarus (Jn 11:43-44). It is totally beyond human experience and so, when it did happen, the first human reaction was fear and trembling, 'They were frightened out of their wits' (Lk 16:8). Part of the prayer of Easter is for fear of the Lord, which is the beginning of wisdom, if the good news is to be preached properly. It is not a servile fear but a filial one.

The disciples are suddenly confronted with a world, which is not what it seems. God the Father, who raised Jesus from the dead (Rom 8:11), is seen and witnessed as more powerful than anything they would have imagined – the power of Rome, the intellectual depth of Greece, the religion of Judaism, even the mighty Temple. This power reduces Jesus' friends to silence and, in a sense, all that they can do is to ponder on the events, which are beyond human comprehension (Lk 2:51b), and let the experiences permeate them. This is perhaps why the post-resurrection prayer is quieter and deeper than the other incidents in Jesus' life. Perhaps we could, in our prayer, ask Mary to help us ponder the events, as she had to do from the beginning of Jesus' life (Lk 2:51b). It was essential for Mary to do this because she didn't understand (v. 50). We, too, need this gift of 'pondering' because we can't understand them either. If we don't, the danger is that we try to 'possess', that is, control these experiences instead of letting them take us over.

It is also due to the fact that his friends are now missing Jesus – 'he had vanished from their sight' (Lk 24:31b). The absence of Jesus, in the sense that he is not there, is also partly due to the relationship they have with him. It takes time for them to assimilate with their hearts (Lk 24:32) the shock of his resurrection and of his absence/presence. So, his appearances and disappearances needed constant repetition for a while so they could understand that he was the 'historical' Jesus yet, at the same time, different. Jesus was trying to deepen their faith. The evangelists showed that this was no easy task as it involved different kinds of his presence e.g. bodily presence

(Lk 24:43); a small group of Christians (Mt 18:19-20); second coming (Mt 16:27); liturgical celebration (Acts 2:46, 1 Cor 11:23-27). Prayer was one of the ways in which they became committed apostles of the resurrection (Acts 1:14). They approached Easter through the heart.

Another way in which they entered into the mystery of Easter was the study of scripture (Lk 24:27), particularly of the prophets, (Acts 2:17, Is 7:19, Mt 3:23-24). In fact, their Christian preaching showed how Jesus fulfilled Old Testament prophecy. They also approached Easter through the head.

It is through these two approaches that they become able to change their Jewish way of living and loving. Paul tells us that the early communities were composed mainly of the marginalised/ social outcasts (1 Cor 4:13). Those 'whom the world thinks common and contemptible are the ones that God has chosen' (1 Cor 1:28). They struggle to survive. Easter means something to be believed and done. They approached Easter through living – usually through touch. Thus, the first friends of Jesus approached Easter through the heart, the head and the hands. Because of this experience, their faith, hope and love gradually became Christianised. Before the resurrection, there was a progression of faith in their knowledge of him: first as Rabbi (Jn 1:38) then

as the Holy One of God (Jn 6:69), finally as the
Messiah (Mk 8:29), yet they are still disillusioned as
they walk along the road to Emmaus (Lk 24:21).

After the resurrection, we have Mary's 'Rabbuni'
(Jn 20:16); 'We have seen the Lord' (Jn 20:25);
Thomas' 'My Lord and My God' (Jn 20:28). Jesus
asks for no better profession of faith from us than
Thomas'. Yet, this transformation in Mary and in
Thomas was the work of the Holy Spirit (Jn 7:39,
16:13, 14:26). Does this mean that Mary of Magdala
received the Holy Spirit before the others (Jn 20:22,
Acts 2:4)? Now, there was no need to look further
than the risen Jesus for God (Jn 14:7-10), because
the Holy Spirit was enlightening their understanding and their faith. Jesus, now risen, has become the
object of universal faith. The resurrection extends
the presence of Jesus and makes it effectively
catholic but is the work of the Holy Spirit (Acts 1:8).
Christian faith is the gift of the Holy Spirit. Do we
ever ask for our faith to be Christianised? Perhaps
we take it for granted (Lk 11:13).

Christian hope is born of this faith in the resurrection. Thomas is blessed but much more so are
those who learn to believe down the ages (Jn 17:20).
Thomas did not believe nor see the divinity with
bodily eyes because faith comes from God the Father
(Mt 16:17), through the Spirit, who has been given

to him and others. Because of the presence of the Spirit within them, the friends of Jesus can witness to his risen life. They have to look to the future as the risen Jesus does in Jn 20:22: the forgiveness of sins, Mt 28:11 (baptism), and so on. Christian hope is the work of the Holy Spirit. We need to ask for the grace of obeying Christ's commandment at the Last Supper: 'Do not let your hearts be troubled. Trust in God still and trust in me' (Jn 14:1).

The Holy Spirit, love itself, permeates the risen Jesus as he progressively reveals himself as a gardener to Mary (Jn 20:16), as a pilgrim to the Emmaus couple (Lk 24:31), using either a word or gesture. In so doing, he gives them back their self-respect: Mary of Magdala, Thomas, Peter, the apostles (Jn 15:12). This enables them, in turn, to pass on Christian love in their mission (Jn 20:21-22), as their risen Master is found in the stranger, the gardener, the friend, the doubter, the insignificant, the lonely and in all created beings (Col 1:16). Christian faith, hope and love are the direct effects of the resurrection and are the foundation of the Christian life. In its light, all that precedes it is only a preparation. We must ask for the realisation that Jesus has been standing at the door of every person's heart since the beginning of time and knocking in different ways and that eventually each person opens out to him (Rev 3:20-21).

CHAPTER SIX

Touch and Reassurance

In chapter 3, we saw that Jesus chose to remain human for ever, to eternalise his human nature. At the moment of death, to the extent we have learnt to love, the humanity of each of us is eternalised. The closer to his father, the closer he wishes to be to his friends. He still needs to be noticed, because like everybody else he remains vulnerable and in need of recognition (Lk 24:31). We should ask the Holy Spirit to help us understand how vulnerable and human Jesus is. He wants to be recognised by his friends, to be touched (Jn 20:27), and how grateful he is to them when they do so. Jesus comes as a gift to them – 'Handle and see, touch and feel, it is really me.' He gives himself and asks for nothing except recognition. Their joy is so great they cannot believe it (Lk 24:41).

Why does Jesus want to be touched? Touching is a very deep form of communication, absolutely essential to an infant if he is to develop normally, to young people, to the sick as well as the healthy. At times, it can communicate more than words such as 'I believe in you', because touching is not just a physical reaching out, but also and above all, an emotional reaching out. Jesus believes in his friends, despite, or maybe because of, their weaknesses. His faith in them demonstrates in action the second great commandment of love (Mk 12:31). A person learns to have faith in himself when others have faith in him and when they show by the different ways in which they demonstrate this love that he is special, indeed unique, that he adds a dimension to their lives that is irreplaceable. By so doing, when an individual comes to believe in himself, he is no longer tempted to self-absorption and he opens himself out to others. It is a form of resurrection, a form of coming alive, because once he starts to believe in himself, he opens up a way of communication, opening out to others. In a certain sense, it is this coming alive that is the good news. Over a period of time, he feels at home with his brothers and sisters in the human family. He starts to co-operate with others in making this world, created by God his Father, into a home; he becomes a homemaker. In turn, he tries to make others feel at home with themselves and with one another by bringing them back to life, by bringing them together in the name of their common Father. This is what everyone is called to do, including Jesus. 'Jesus grew in maturity and grace before his Father and others' (Lk 2:52). Part of our Easter prayer should be to ask that we might also become homemakers (Jn 15:4).

But it is not just people a person touches and transforms, it is also the material world around him (Gen 1:28-31). God the Father needs co-workers to care for his earth and all that it contains, which he made and saw was very good (Gen 2:5b). We have to become stewards of this creation and help to make it into a home. Nature is a gift to be received with admiration and gratitude (Dan 3:57-88). Nature desires us to hear and see the great story of the Father's love to which it points. Jesus says, 'Look and see' for the flowers, the birds, the grass will invite us to become more open and more human because, through them, Jesus' Father touches us in the same way as the world and other people do (Mt 6:26). The flowers are not God, neither is the grass nor the birds, but to open out to them is to find Emmanuel, God-with-us. We need to ask the Holy Spirit to Christianise our faith, hope and love to help us discern the presence of God in all things (Jn 20:8), and in all people (Jn 20:16). We also need to ask for help for us to believe in the ministry of nature so we do not restrict our ministry just to people (Gen 1:25). These post-resurrection scenes show us that plants and animals as well as people tell us of the great love of God the Father (Lk 8:5).

Again, touching can be a reaching out in the form of a reassuring gesture. First of all, Jesus gets reassurance from his Father as he brings Jesus back to life, 'Well done, thou good and faithful servant, enter into the joy of the Lord.' He is his Father and so he needs him (Rom 8:11). What father would not want his only son to be at home with him? Secondly, Jesus gets reassurance from his apostles. Once Thomas has rejoined the community, Jesus asks him to touch him. We're not told whether he actually physically touched him but Thomas' response was, 'My Lord and My God' (Jn 20:28). In consequence Jesus could reply, 'You believe because you can see me.' Jesus was reassured because true love, although it doesn't seek a response, is completed when it gets one.

After breakfast with his apostles at the lake of Tiberias, Jesus puts an unusual question to Peter (Jn 21:15), 'Do you love me more than these others?' Most of us would hesitate to ask for this reassurance of our friends yet Jesus asks it of Peter. Overt signs of affection are necessary between human friends and they are just as necessary in our relationship with God the Father, because they are indications of our desire to love him. Jesus asked this question because it was important to him. Part of the great mystery of Easter is Jesus' need for his friends. How mysterious, in some ways, this is. His need for them rather than their need for him. Peter is being told that he will not be effective unless he loves and that is why he is asked the question three times. The reassurance is given and Jesus gives joy, hope and life, not only to Peter, but also to all his friends.

The same question, 'Do you love me more than these others?' is asked of us too (Jn 21:17). Let us ask the Holy Spirit to give Jesus the reassurance that our moods, our troubles, are insignificant compared to the call of love, which is the first Christian calling. We are merely returning the love first given to us (1 Jn 4:10-11), and, in the end, it is the only thing that matters.

CHAPTER SEVEN

Easter Joy

Jesus showed us the depths of his love by laying down his life for his friends (Jn 15:13). He wanted them to be able to communicate with a living person, so he rose again to be with his friends. Like us, the disciples are not merely imitating a dead hero. They are united to a living Christ (1 Cor 15:17-19) and through him they will come to understand that they are united to a living God (Jn 6:44).

During his mortal life he learned from John the Baptist (Mt 3:13), who described himself as the 'best man at a wedding' (Jn 3:29-30). A 'best man' usually has a good relationship with the bridegroom. During the celebrations, he works to make sure everything is just right. He is joyful in doing it, giving no thought to himself. This is an example of true joy for the sake and happiness of somebody else. He is content to stand aside and let the couple be in the limelight. This is what Jesus is trying to do in order to allow us to develop a relationship with God.

A person who loves deeply wants to share every-

thing and it was natural for Jesus to appear to his
friends so he could share with them his Easter joy.
Jesus' friends were sad, perhaps even devastated by
his cruel death, their weaknesses and by the way
they betrayed Jesus (Lk 24:17). There may, however,
have been an element of selfishness, or self-pity in
that sadness. They would need to set this aside if
they were to rejoice with him in his triumph. It
must be his joy, and it should be our prayer 'that we
may live no longer for ourselves but for him'
(*Eucharistic Prayer* 4). Joy, which is the fruit of the
Holy Spirit, permeated Jesus' mortal life and transformed the humble, human joys of life into something much deeper: he found joy in the birds of the
air (Mt 6:26, 28), the flowers of the field, a man
finding a treasure (Mt 13:44), a father embracing a
son returning from a prodigal life (Lk 15:22-24), a
woman bringing a son into the world (Jn 16:21-22).
For Jesus, these are spiritual joys of the kingdom of
God (Jn 1:3). He accepted and experienced human
and spiritual joys as a gift from his Father. We,
unfortunately, are so poor in this respect that we
must beg, pray to the Holy Spirit to open our eyes
to the joys of the kingdom in ordinary things. We
are, usually, so possessive that we dominate them
instead of being their stewards.

At Easter, Jesus' human nature was eternalised forever and so his joy through his suffering, death and resurrection (Mt 5:11-12), also become an integral part of him forever. On Calvary, there were still a few faithful followers, some women and John (Jn 19:25-27). However, at the resurrection, no one was there, not even Mary, and Jesus had to convert all of them, one by one, to his joy. He needed the Holy Spirit, the Comforter, to help him (Jn 20:22) and he needed his friends to overcome their sorrow and come alive again.

This gift of the resurrection, which Jesus received from his Father, was now passed on to his friends (2 Cor 1:4). He enlivened them through his joy. As well as joy, Jesus' friends need the Holy Spirit, the Comforter at this time. This is true of us too, we need her as Comforter, if we are going to be true witnesses of his resurrection. Easter does not merely bring death, Easter also brings the gift of life (Jn 10:10). Easter joy is the fruit of love poured into our hearts (Rom 5:5) and Jesus came to show the depth of his Father's love for us (Jn 3:16); nevertheless he also wills the cross for us (Jn 15:13-14).

This seems contradictory. It is very significant that Jesus speaks of his joy to his friends during his passion (Jn 12:20-21), because the joy of the fruitfulness of his death brings about reconciliation (Eph 2:15-16). They become not only reconciled with other people but also with his Father. When Jesus showed his friends his hands and his side, the marks of his crucifixion (Jn 20:20), they were filled with joy at seeing him. They knew by the way they looked at him that they were forgiven for deserting him in his hour of need. There was no recrimination, only a looking forward (v. 21). In this way, he restored their self-respect and gave to his repentant friends a new power of selflessness. Their experience of Easter joy gives them an awareness of the forgiveness of God and a desire to pass this on to others. In our relationships with others, do we bear witness to this Easter joy when reconciliation takes place? Only the Holy Spirit, both as Comforter and as Joy, can give us the desire and the ability to pass it on to others. Let us pray for this gift.

Christian joy cannot be totally equated with human joy. Christian joy should suggest a sadness overcome, the sadness of saying 'No' to Jesus. We tend to be well aware of our failures, of lost innocence, of darkness of heart. We are good at brooding about ourselves; we have forgotten how to laugh at ourselves! If we human beings cannot laugh at ourselves, perhaps it is because we have lost our 'inner' freedom. When we give up God, or give up spending time with him in prayer, we become too serious. God is joy! Faith in God suggests that there is something beyond sorrow; it suggests that sorrow can lead to joy. The life and death of Jesus bears witness to this. No Christian will ever explain rationally why the Father sent his Son. There is no other convincing reason for Easter or Pentecost except to demonstrate God's love for us. Easter shows that sorrow is not the end. God the Father made us for celebration (Gen 1:26-31). We were created to celebrate and be messengers of joy in this world, a world which has gradually become obsessed with gloom. Only an experience of Christian peace and joy can counteract this negativity, and this is why the risen Jesus commanded his friends and us to bring peace and joy to others (Mt 28:18-20). Once again, we can only obtain this through prayer, such as, for example, the prayer used on the Sixth Sunday of Easter:

> Ever living Father,
> help us to celebrate our joy,
> in the resurrection of the Lord
> and to express in our lives,
> the love we celebrate.

CHAPTER EIGHT

Easter Maker

Jesus showed the depths of his love by laying down his life for his friends (Jn 15:13), yet we can only communicate with someone whom we believe is still alive. Jesus is love and out of love he rose to be with his friends once more (1 Cor 15:17-19). Just like his friends, we ask his Father, the Spirit of the risen Christ, for the gift to understand by faith, not by reason, that the end and goal of our lives is to be risen, to be with him.

But Easter is not confined to the 'resurrection on the last day'. It keeps happening. We need to understand it as a historical fact but, more important, we need to be attuned to the presence of the risen Lord in our daily lives.

While the resurrection is about the risen Jesus, it also concerns his followers. The recognition that the risen Jesus was Son of God the Father was the power that transformed the early community; it changed the disillusioned and disaffected followers of Jesus into a restored people, forming communities in which the racial differences of Jew and non-Jew might be overcome. This recognition was expressed in a variety of gifts, above all in the way people shared their possessions with one another (Acts 2:44-47). This recognition built up and nurtured people; it enabled the 'marginalised', as Paul described them, to remain hopeful throughout their suffering and persecution (Lk 24:26). It enabled people to forgive others as they themselves had been forgiven. The resurrection is therefore not merely an abstract idea. Unless we try to create an environment in which our faith can be expressed, the world will not open itself out to the power of the risen Jesus. A community which sees death as final offers no hope, as the angel said on the first Easter morning (Lk 24:5) or as Jesus said, 'Let the dead bury the dead'. Easter is the feast when we celebrate a God who refuses to leave the dead forever dead. Jesus suffered a violent death and was buried (Jn 19:41-42), but God his Father had no intention of letting Jesus rest in peace! Whenever therefore we take God's part in protesting against death in the midst of life, a 'culture of death', as Pope John Paul describes it, for example, against abortion or euthanasia, against violence and suffering or in challenging hopeless and helpless feelings about the ability to change our lives, we become Easter-makers. Asking for this gift should be part of our petitionary prayer during Eastertide, for only the Holy Spirit of the risen Christ can effect it in our lives.

As a friendship unfolds, our eyes are opened. We 'see', not so much with the physical eyes, but with the eyes of faith, with the love we have for another (Eph 1:17-18). Friendship is about one person opening out to another, giving ourself to our friend and forgetting ourselves (Phil 2:5ff). Through friendship, we become more human, more ourselves. In valuing our friend, we bring our friend to life. This is a kind of resurrection (Jn 11:41-44). In this way we are Easter-makers. Every time we bring love and friendship to another, or bring joy to someone who is feeling low or downcast, perhaps just by greeting him in the morning, or saying 'you look well' or 'it's great to see you' we are Easter-makers. When we listen and allow somebody to express the depth of his fear, worry or confusion (Mt 28:10), we are acting in the spirit of the risen Lord, who did the same. We are Easter-makers and enable Easter to keep happening.

To be an Easter-maker it is not enough just to offer words of comfort or reassurance. It is not enough just to listen or to put an arm around the shoulder when a friend is upset. To be like the risen

Jesus, to console like the Jesus, we have to join them in their suffering whatever suffering that may be, and to lead them through that suffering to something greater; to lead our friend to a resurrection. That is Easter-making. When our friend is worried or anxious, fearing the worst, then discovers all is well, they feel better, physically as well as mentally, they can relax, they can eat and sleep again. Similarly, when a person is feeling a bit low, unappreciated and unloved and then finds they are needed, they get a new zest for living. Such incidents may seem small in themselves but, for the individual concerned, they are significant; moments that lift the spirits up and bring about a mini-resurrection for them. To bring about a resurrection in someone is to call the person to faith, greater faith than before and to a new challenge. It gives the person a new mission, another chance to begin again. To bring about a mini-resurrection in someone is to show faith in their ability to come alive and to give life to others, to inspire them with hope. It's as if Jesus is saying 'they can come back to life, too'.

There is an ancient story of a Rabbi, who gathered his students together early one morning. While it was still dark, he asked them how they could tell that night had ended and the day was on its way. He

got various answers such as: 'when one could distin-
guish between the different types of animals, or
different types of trees'. Eventually, they asked him
for the answer. He replied, 'It is when you look on
the face of any man or woman and see that he is
your brother and she is your sister. If you cannot do
this, then, no matter what time it is you are still in
the dark.' What he describes is how to become an
Easter-maker. Easter begins in the dark and in the
tomb. An example of this is someone whom many
Jews had written off as worthless, Mary of Magdala.
Once Jesus, the despised criminal, conquers death,
nobody can be written off as worthless again. Easter
faith challenges us always to see more in others than
'meets the eye' (Jn 20:16, Lk 24:31), their potential,
not just their feelings.

We spend many hours each week talking about
what has happened to us. The disciples, who tried
to retreat to Emmaus after the crucifixion and who
were restored to life by Jesus, shared their experience with their friends (Lk 24:35). Whenever people
come together to share good memories, Jesus is
present. Whenever people come together to be life-
giving, the risen Lord is present (Mt 18:20). When
Mary of Magdala met Jesus in the garden disguised
as a gardener, she recognised him when he said her

name, 'Mary'. When he told her not to cling to him, he was calling her to be an Easter-maker. 'Do not cling to me as you formerly knew and loved me … go and find my brothers and sisters and there you will discover me in the way I wish to be present to you' (Jn 20:17). This is our call, too. We are called to be peacemakers, to make Jesus alive to other people, and so our prayer might be 'Here I am, Lord, send me' (Is 6:9).

CHAPTER NINE

Mary of Magdala: Watching in silence

There is a silence, very early in the morning, when darkness seems to encourage stillness and listening, when the world is still sleeping, and there is no visible activity (Wis 18:14). This stillness of man and nature helps us to enter into the prayer of Easter, the prayer of silence and waiting. It is the silence of the night awaiting the dawn and emerging activity. Prayer seems to come quite naturally to us when stillness calms the mind and heart. Perhaps this quiet time helps us to recognise that, ultimately, we are vulnerable and alone. Perhaps this is what moves Mary of Magdala as she journeys to the tomb of Jesus: she feels alone and vulnerable (v. 1). She feels alone and bewildered by recent events. Jesus had helped her to move through darkness and despair (Lk 8:2), into light. He knew her past and, by forgiving her, he brought her back to life. She is thrown back into the darkness. The darkness of the night somehow makes loneliness or worry even more intense. At such a time it is easy to believe the worst. Nevertheless Mary of Magdala went on loving and believing even when she could not understand.

As was the custom, she was visiting the tomb of her dead friend three days after the body had been laid there. It was thought that during these three days, the spirit of the loved one hovered around the tomb, but that on the fourth day, the spirit departed, as the body began to decompose (Jn 11:39). Since the Sabbath fell on one of these three days, Mary of Magdala could not visit the tomb. It would have broken the religious laws. She had to wait until the first day of the week, Sunday. Although full of despair, love urged her on (Song. 3:1). Her pain was not like that of the apostles, the pain of guilt, it was the pure pain of loss. She had lost her sense of being loved (Jn 31:3), of being valued and of being given meaning. This pain of loss was deepened when she arrived to find the stone removed. Not only was she not able to fulfil the funeral rites for her friend, but the thought that the guard had disappeared allowing the Jews to break the seal on the stone (Mt 27:66) and to desecrate Jesus' body, shocked her. The first emotions of the resurrection experience for Mary were shock, horror and fear. Since this was the first reaction of Jesus' friends, perhaps in our prayer we should ask to share some of these emotions, as otherwise we might well lose the full impact of the Easter experience.

Another element of our prayer might be to ask for some understanding of God the Father's ways (Is 55:8-9), because it is not easy to grasp the way he chooses to proclaim his Son's resurrection. At that time the testimony of a woman could not have had the same weight as the testimony of a man. In addition, why was Peter not the first to see Jesus after the resurrection? Peter seems to have been the acknowledged leader of the disciples, in spite of his public denial (Mk 14:7). He had not fled with the others but had remained near at hand during Jesus' interrogation by the Jewish authorities (Lk 22:61). Peter retained a certain moral strength and status. Jesus had discerned this in him when he chose him as leader,(Jn 15:16). With typical impulsiveness, Peter did not merely look into the tomb, as John did. He went in, looked around. He saw the grave clothes, lying there undisturbed.

John, the one whom Jesus loved, was present throughout Jesus' passion (Jn 13:23-25); he was at the Last Supper leaning on Jesus' breast (Jn 18:15-16). He followed Jesus into the High Priest's house. Finally, he was at the crucifixion (Jn 19:26-27), when Jesus placed his mother into his care. Bewildered, like

Mary of Magdala, deep loss urged him on and he was the first to believe in the resurrection of Jesus. He believed in the risen Jesus before he saw him because of the winding clothes he saw in the tomb. Earlier on (Jn 11:44), we were told that Lazarus came forth from the tomb 'bound hand and foot with linen strips and his face wrapped in cloth'. Jesus left his wrappings behind in the tomb. Lazarus was to die again (Jn 12:6), and so would need his burial garments again. The garments left by Jesus, on the other hand, revealed to the Beloved Disciple that Jesus had been raised to eternal life. This faith in the resurrection came more easily to him because his love for Jesus had made him very sensitive to him. His love for Jesus gave him the ability to detect his presence (v. 8). Somehow, however, he did not seem to be able to pass this faith on to Peter or Mary, and he and Peter left the scene.

Mary was left, solitary and alone in her grief, still waiting and watching.

CHAPTER TEN

Jesus appears to Mary of Magdala
(John 20:11-18)

To love is to communicate with somebody who is loving and so, in one sense, Jesus had to rise again to be with his friends. In this way, we, his friends of today, are also united to the risen Jesus. As Paul says (1 Cor 15:17-19), we are strengthened by our friendship with Jesus who is alive and working through us (Eph 3:20). This communication is a deeper level of presence and influence than he had with his apostles during his mortal life and this dynamic power, emanating from him, diffuses peace and security. Yet it can feel 'arid', because it is communicated in the 'seeming' absence of Jesus.

Mary, for example, goes off to look for him, but to no avail. This makes her all the more determined to find him. He draws Mary to him by giving her the desire to seek him, yet at first she doesn't get what she wants. The empty tomb echoes the emptiness of her heart, and she feels nothing but the pain of loss. The temptation is self-absorption, to think of nothing but her loss.

Jesus, in all the post-resurrection passages, appears among his friends as 'Another'. Then their attention – here Mary's attention – is no longer absorbed in herself but is drawn towards 'only Jesus'. The attention gradually annihilates the tendency to self-absorption. Her love starts to become universal (Jn 21:12). Thus one aspect of the post-resurrection prayer is to find God's presence in all things and in all people. John saw the hand of God in the clothes left behind in the tomb and Mary found Jesus in the gardener (Jn 20:8, 16).

In v. 16, he gradually leads her and all his friends to a 'cosmic' dimension of his risen existence. He has changed his relationship with them and also with us because he is risen. Next to Peter, James and John, Mary of Magdala is the most frequently mentioned gospel follower of Jesus. On her second visit to the tomb, it doesn't say whether it was still dark or light. Darkness is normally associated with the absence of Jesus and light is normally associated with his presence (Jn 21:4). It is physically dark; it also feels like a 'dark moment' because she believes that the worst has happened. Despite the presence of the angels, one at the head and the other at the feet, Mary's remains desolate (vv. 11-13). Mary is buried in the past. Everything seems bleak. The reality is quite the opposite. Mary of Magdala weeps profoundly and does not hear the angels say, 'Why are you weeping?' because she is totally desolate. Could tears have blurred her vision? Similarly she fails to recognise Jesus, whom she mistakes for the gardener. Perhaps she does not recognise him because she is still facing in the wrong direction, towards the empty tomb and her back turned towards Jesus?

Why did it take Mary so long to recognise Jesus? Perhaps Paul gives us a clue. He explains that the resurrection is a combination of continuity and transformation (1 Cor 15:42-44). Jesus died and his body was buried. Now it is no longer physical but spiritual. The gospel accounts do bring out these two aspects: continuity as emphasised in the stories of the empty tomb and transformation by the recognition scenes. 'In your light, let us see light' could be part of our prayer now because it is only in the light, infused by the Holy Spirit, that we ever see people as images of God. We see how Mary needed this light, when she saw a gardener instead of recognising Jesus.

Touch is a gesture of re-assurance and friendship. Yet he tells Mary 'Do not cling to me.' Jesus is telling Mary that although he has returned, he is no longer the one she knew. She needs to realise this. If she clings to the old Jesus, she will not understand the richness of his presence with her now. This presence now comes through the gift of his Spirit, which is the Spirit of the God-made-man, who can come only once he has ascended to be with his Father (Jn 16:7). In this way, the power to become one of God's children (Jn 1:12a) is fulfilled for her. Once she understands this she is able to bring the good news of the fatherhood of God to others, especially to his close friends. In this way too (Jn 1:12a), we all have the power to become God's children.

In a sense, Mary's story is everyone's story. For each of us, it sometimes feels as if Jesus has abandoned us but, like Mary, all we need to do is wait if we are experiencing an 'arid' period in our prayer. What must we wait for? We must wait until Jesus reveals himself to us.

CHAPTER ELEVEN

Jesus appears to the apostles
(Luke 24:36-43, John 20:19-23)

These narratives are all good examples of God the Father, extending his hand in friendship to us through his risen Son, Jesus. He seeks out the holy women, the apostles, and eventually runs after the Emmaus disciples. This is the kind of Father he is, a Father who seeks his lost sheep (Lk 15:3-4).

Does he seek his friends out in the busy streets of Jerusalem or in the Temple? He prefers to look for them on a quiet country road, or by a lakeside, or in a locked room. It is not that he cannot be with them in the busy city, but like us, he is so pushed around by the crowds that they cannot get near him. His voice gets dimmed by the noise of the crowd around them, with the result that they cannot hear him distinctly. They get drawn to the babble of some of the crowd instead of hearing his voice (Jn 10:3-5). Like them, we need a quiet environment to meet Jesus. It is necessary to meet Jesus in this way because he has to reach us – not through physical walls (Jn 20:19, Lk 24:36), but through the barriers we have created in our minds, the barriers of our prejudice (Rev 3:20). When we meet Jesus, there is a confrontation because he demands a response from us, a 'yes' or a 'no'. St John and St Luke have different descriptions of the same situation. We will look at St Luke first and then fill in with other details from St John.

The disciples are all gathered together for several reasons: they have let down Jesus, their friend, by abandoning him when he was arrested and they let one another down, because each ran away to save himself. Now, they are afraid of Jesus (Lk 24:36-43). In addition, they are afraid of the hostility of the Jews. It feels as if there is no one to turn to. They are turned in on themselves like the closed doors of a room. Only love can open them out and this is what the risen Jesus does for them. When Jesus appears (v. 36) they are unmoved because they think he is a ghost – they do not know how much he loves them. Like the Pharisees, they have not understood Jesus' dying words, 'Father, forgive them for they know not what they do' (Lk 23:34). They do not know how much he loved them. They did not realise how much he needed them (Jn 6:67). Sometimes, when we pray this passage, we could consider the immense power of God the Father which will enter into our lives if we but open out to him.

Jesus constantly comes to us because he loves us. If he says 'come', then we must open the doors of our hearts. If we have difficulties in prayer, we must always ask ourselves: 'Am I open to the Holy Spirit; to my brothers and sisters in Christ? Is the door to my heart wide or is it just slightly ajar?' If we are really open, then we are really praying and the Holy Spirit is within us, because only love can teach us to pray. Often our hearts are controlled by insecurity and fear. Jesus tells us 'Fear not!' He wants us to be at peace. This has always been Jesus' attitude, but it takes time for the disciples to realise that Jesus is the healer of the sick and that often it is we who are sick. We could use as our prayer the message Martha and Mary sent to Jesus (Jn 11:3), 'Lord, he whom you love is ill' (Pray this phrase but substitute 'he' with your own name.)

Peace and joy emanate from the appearance of the risen Jesus because he is now able to grant the gift of the Holy Spirit, the Spirit of the God-made-man, the Spirit of the crucified and risen Lord. (See Chapter 18 on Pentecost). Jesus emphasises the continuity between the crucifixion and resurrection by showing his friends his hands and feet. This gift of the Holy Spirit is the only way they can have his 'enduring presence and his peace' (Jn 14:26-28). The transformation from a 'state of alarm, of fright because they thought they had seen a ghost', to one of unbounded joy is the work of the Spirit of the risen Jesus. We should always ask the Holy Spirit to help us to realise the powerful effect of the resurrection on the apostles, because we might find it difficult to be in a state of fear. If we do not feel fear, then we might miss out on the full impact of Easter joy (Jn 16:22). Life takes on another dimension once we have been re-established like them: 'Touch me and see for yourselves; a ghost has no flesh and bones as you can see I have' (v. 39). As Paul shows us, there has to be a quality of peace to their calling (Eph 2:14-18). We, too, will require this peace if we are to see the risen Jesus. If we are not at peace, we ourselves will be in the way. We never see others clearly unless we have the kind of faith the risen Jesus has in his friends. He sees people not just as they are but also as the people they could become. It is Jesus' faith in us, not our faith in him, that makes us an Easter people.

Perhaps the crisis of today is not one of doctrine but one of faith in one another. Do we really appreciate what we lose when a friend dies? Perhaps we assess our friends by our very narrow criteria because we are used to very shallow relationships.

We don't really have much faith in our friends. The Priestly Prayer (Jn 17), is an illustration of how much faith Jesus has in his friends, even at the very time they are about to betray him. He is willing to take the risk of trusting them (Jn 17:12). Our faith would be stronger if we, too, could come to believe in those we feel might let us down (Mt 5:44-45).

As we saw earlier, Easter keeps happening. People come to life when they meet those who believe in them (Lk 24:41). 'What proves that the Father loves us is that his Son died for us when we were still sinners' (Rom 5:8). Even after physical death, it is God our Father's power to believe in us that brings us to life again (Rom 8:11). Like the apostles, we must ask for the grace to enter into the mystery of Easter by which another is reborn. Jesus is not so much risen from the dead when he leaves the tomb, but clearly is when he stands in the circle of those who see him, and who are brought back to life by his Spirit.

Instead of merely paying lip service, if we really believe in others we will be able to proclaim whole-heartedly: 'Christ is risen, Alleluia!' We could now turn to St John's account to fill in more details. The apostles were all gathered in the upper room because they had heard what the women had reported. They may well not have believed the women but they did believe Peter and the disciples who had returned from Emmaus. They were all afraid and disconsolate because of what they had done. They had closed the doors because they feared the hostility of the Jews but they were also apprehensive of the Lord, because they had let him down. They had no one else to turn to. They were full of fears and doubts and closed in on themselves.

It is evening which means darkness, and this darkness represents not just physical darkness but also the ignorance of the disciples. They did not realise that Jesus was coming to them as the light of the world, to be accepted by some and rejected by others (Jn 1:10-12). He has to penetrate the closed doors of their minds and hearts with 'Peace be with you'. True peace requires me to be at peace with myself, with others and with God, but I cannot do this without the Spirit of the risen Jesus.

When Jesus appeared, the disciples were not immediately affected. They felt he could not restore peace of mind to them because they had let him down. They had not appreciated how much he loved them. This is why Jesus needed them to feel at peace. They were not at peace with God, with other people or with themselves. They needed the peace of the Holy Spirit to restore their peace of mind after they had 'let him down'. They were worried about what he would say to them. His desire was merely to restore their trust in him. The Holy Spirit could heal them and then restore their faith in one another. They would become 'one mind and one heart' and, as we saw earlier, it is from this that true reconciliation comes.

Only when we are really at peace with ourselves will we be able to accept other people as they are and also to help them to grow. This is the peace Jesus brings to the disciples. It is so important when praying this passage that we accept ourselves as we are 'warts and all', but recognise that we still have to grow in love. Jesus shows his hands and his side to his disciples. The resurrection does not mean the marks of cruelty and suffering disappear. The risen Jesus is the Jesus who was crucified and died. There must always be honesty in our prayer.

'Jesus breathed on them' (Jn 20:22). In so doing, Jesus gave the disciples the gift of the Holy Spirit to make them peaceful and joyful. This is the high-point of his appearances to his friends. Just as God the Father breathed his breath into man and made him a living being (Gen 2:7, Wis 15:11), so now, in the moment of the new creation, the risen Jesus breathed his own Spirit into his friends and gave them eternal life (Jn 17:6). Without the Holy Spirit, his disciples and friends could not appreciate the whole truth about Jesus and his Father. They came to that truth now (Jn 14:26) and this enabled them to see themselves in a new light and this changed the direction of their lives. All they wanted now was to follow in his footsteps. Only when they had received the Spirit of truth were they able to answer the question, 'Who do you say that I am?' (Mt 16:15). They had a newfound identity and a new direction to their lives. Now they were ready to be sent out to the world to proclaim the good news, because they were seeing things with 'new' minds (Rom 12:2). This allowed them to be sensitive to the real needs of other people, to find the Father's presence in other people.

God sent his Son Jesus, whose name means Saviour (Mk 1:21), on a mission of reconciliation, reconciling everyone with God his Father and then with one another. Now the disciples have been reconciled with Jesus and through him with their Father. It is once they are reconciled themselves that Jesus can send them out to pass on what they, themselves have experienced (Acts 2:38-39).

It is only now that Jesus can give them the power

to forgive sin. They could not forgive sin of their own accord. Only Jesus, working through them can do it. They forgave sins in the name of Jesus Christ. The words of absolution state:

God the Father of mercies
Through the death and resurrection of his Son
Has reconciled the world to himself
And sent the Holy Spirit among us
For the forgiveness of sins;
Through the ministry of the church
May God give you pardon and peace.
And I absolve you from your sins
In the name of the Father and of the Son
And of the Holy Spirit. Amen.

Reconciliation was the reason for the existence of this small community which would grow into what we now call the church. It was a reconciling community. This group of people would attempt to bring over not so much a verbal message but a person, the risen Jesus himself, who shed his blood 'for you and for all so that sins may be forgiven. Do this in memory of me.' (These are the words of consecration.)

St Paul explains it beautifully (2 Cor 5:20): 'We are ambassadors for Christ; it is as though God were appealing through us and the appeal that we make in Christ's name is: be reconciled to God.' This means that we, like those disciples in the upper room, must receive the Spirit of the risen Jesus. This puts a heavy responsibility on all of us for two reasons. Firstly, it shows how vulnerable Jesus is to our response, since Paul says, 'It is as though God were appealing through us.' God the Father appeals to us to use our personalities and our experience of being forgiven ourselves, to pass reconciliation on to others. Without us, in some way or other, God the Father's plan is thwarted. Secondly, just as Jesus' forgiveness of sin forces a person to repent or deliberately remain in sin (Jn 9:39-41), so, when the disciples forgive in Jesus' name, people judge themselves. They have the choice to repent or not to repent. They will choose either to come into the light and seek forgiveness, or turn away and be hardened in their sin. We are today's disciples of Jesus and perhaps our prayer to help others could be that of Solomon, 'Give your servant a heart to understand how to discern between good and evil, for who could govern this people of yours that is so great?' (1 Kings 3:9).

CHAPTER TWELVE

Jesus appears to Thomas

In a certain sense, the resurrection is not so much about Jesus as about his followers. Certainly, there is continuity of Jesus from his mortal life and also a discontinuity, but, according to Paul, it is foolish for us to try and understand exactly what has happened (1 Cor 15:35ff). Jesus is still present in the flesh because he is not a spirit or a ghost (Lk 24:39). Jesus' continually invites us to 'look, touch and see'. Somehow, his presence is different as the risen Jesus comes through locked doors. In some way, Jesus is transformed.

One of the strongest proofs of the resurrection is the transformation seen in his friends. They experienced the forgiveness of their own sins and so began sharing their possessions with one another (Acts 2:44-47), and forming communities in which the racial differences of Jew and Geek were eradicated. They transformed their daily lives, especially the way they lived. Part of the prayer of the resurrection is to ask for the grace to allow that transforming power into our own lives and into our families: to ask for the faith that our mortal bodies and material world will be transformed beyond our imaginings (1 Cor 2:9). Unless we try to create an environment in which such faith can be expressed, then the world will not open out to the power of the risen Jesus. An environment closed in on death offers no hope, as the angel said on the first Easter morning (Lk 24:5). The resurrection gathered disillusioned and disaffected followers of Jesus into a restored people. One of the best examples of this was Thomas, who went from disbelief to belief.

St John is perhaps unique in the gospel accounts because he pays so much attention to one person's search for the risen Christ. Mary Magdalene looked for his body and when she was found by the risen Christ she was content. Thomas, however, was different because he personified doubt with his first reaction to the risen Jesus. He represents all those who were not present with the disciples on Easter evening (Jn 1:39). Jesus challenges John and Andrew to 'come and see' and so they bring others to Jesus. Jesus' invitation to come and see who he is, is now fulfilled and they can say (Jn 20:25): 'We have seen the Lord.' This is what the other disciples said to Thomas. They had spent Easter Sunday evening,

not with their mortal friend, but with the risen
Lord. Thomas denied this. It is the new faith that
demonstrates the resurrection. The empty tomb was
of no consequence to the apostles after the risen
Jesus' appearances. This rejection by Thomas would
be a typical response to the good news.

Why did Thomas have misgivings? Thomas is
chosen to be an apostle and given his instructions
along with the other eleven (Mt 10:3). There is no
doubt that he, like the others, wants to serve people.
He is, however, perhaps sharper than the others and
sees that Jesus' mission is going to end in failure. He
senses, for example, that by returning to Jerusalem,
Jesus is going to die, 'We are martyrs to a lost cause'
(Jn 11:16). Thomas has a grim loyalty to Jesus and
doggedly does not give up. His reaction to defeat is
morose. Thomas, however, does not lack courage, as
he was willing to go to Jerusalem to die with Jesus,
while the rest of the apostles hesitated (Jn 11:12). His
pessimism and a questioning attitude tended to
undermine morale.

Thomas is known as the 'twin'. He has a dual
personality. On the one hand, he seems to have lost
his faith in Jesus. 'Lord, we do not know where you
are going so how can we know the way?' (Jn 14:15).
On the other hand he still longs for his early fervour.

He is confused. A struggle is going on inside himself. All this perhaps made him the 'odd man out' among the apostles, and so he is not with them when Jesus appears. He is not with them, not only physically but also not 'with them' in faith. Faith is normally caught from other people and so he becomes a loner, rejecting their good news (Jn 20:25). Thomas was a loner in that he sought loneliness rather than togetherness in his sorrow and because he was not with his friends, he missed the first coming of Jesus. Given his temperament, faith was never an easy thing for Thomas. He had to be sure for he had to count the cost. However, empirical facts such as touching Jesus' hands and side prove nothing, because belief in a person does not come from scientific proof. Thomas' problem is that he is hanging on to the past, the passion, when Easter has already changed everything. He is living in the dark past and is blind to the beaming present. He could not get over the passion and so lost contact with the other apostles. It makes him incapable of accepting the surprise of the resurrection and its intense joy.

The risen Jesus waits for Thomas to return to the community because when he does return he is ready for healing. Jesus realises Thomas is still immersed in the passion, and shows him he is no longer in the

wounds of the passion. He is now in the wounds of
his glorified body. These wounds are now an essential
part of the resurrection. Thomas had thought that
the passion was the end of Jesus (Lk 24:26).

Thomas had doubted his friends' good news but
he would have loved to be able to believe them.
After all, they had all let Jesus down and deserted
him at the moment of his greatest need. They had
all refused to believe in the women's story (Lk 24:11).
It would be unfair just to criticise Thomas for not
believing. They all had their doubts. Thomas could
never still his doubts but perhaps what separated
him from the rest of the group was his commitment
to the truth. Thomas stands both for those who
have not seen the Lord and are asked to believe in
him and for all those who honestly doubt and are
seeking the truth.

At the time of Thomas' doubt, he had not been
given the Spirit of the risen Jesus, the Spirit of Truth
(v. 22), which was only given on Easter Sunday
evening. He was still trying to establish the truth
about Jesus' appearance. Thomas' honesty shows
itself when he actually sees Jesus because the
accounts suggest he did not literally put his hands
into Jesus' side; seeing Jesus was enough for him.
Just as Thomas is fearless in expressing his doubts,

he is quick to proclaim his faith, and indeed he makes the deepest affirmation of faith, 'My Lord and my God.' When he sees the truth he goes the whole way. Although love does not seek recognition, it does need it if it is to be complete. Jesus needs Thomas' recognition if their love is to be complete and this happens when Thomas makes his tremendous act of adoration, 'My Lord and my God.' Part of our prayer is to ask to realise how vulnerable the risen Jesus is to our recognising who he is, how human Jesus remains even after the resurrection.

There is a contemporary ring about Thomas' demands to see the holes in Jesus' hands and to put his hands into his side. Thomas cannot actually see the divinity of Jesus, yet he responds 'My Lord and my God.' Jesus' words 'put your finger here … your hand there … doubt no longer but believe' are commandments that apply to all of us (Jn 15:15), because fundamentally we are all like Thomas. We find the passion and death of Jesus hard. It is not the way we do things or the way we would bring the Father's friendship to others. Jesus had to convert the apostles to his way of thinking (Is 55:8-9):

'Yes, the heavens are as high above the earth
As my ways are above your ways,
My thoughts above your thoughts'.

He had to change their way of thinking (Mt 16:23), which is also ours. That is why our prayer must be that of the father of the epileptic boy, 'I do have faith. Help the little faith I have.' (Mk 9:24). If we open ourselves out like Thomas, out of our doubt, Jesus can draw out an act of faith and love; out of our ignorance, he can draw an act of knowledge and love; out of our insecurity, he can draw security. If we admit our doubts and failures, our desire to do better, then the power of the resurrection cannot but be operative in us.

Finally there is the beatitude which is a 'bridge between those who saw Jesus and those who did not'. As long as Jesus lived, a man or woman came to faith through the senses. This is what happened to Peter, John, Thomas (Mt 13:16). Yet seeing is not necessarily believing. The apostles were essential to the church, as were the women who first witnessed the resurrection, as was Mary, his mother as witness to his childhood. They all saw, believed and carried out the mission entrusted to them (Jn 17:19). However, as Jesus told his friends, with the end of his appearances, there dawns the era of the Holy Spirit (Jn 16:7-8). The era of the signs and appearances is passing away but another era begins, namely that of the Holy Spirit. The Spirit enables a person who has not seen Jesus to believe in him. Jesus says in Jn 20:29b: 'Happy are those who have not seen yet believe.' Part of our prayer should be to thank all those who have passed on this faith to us through the power of the Holy Spirit and have made us aware of our responsibility to do the same (Jn 17:20). The last words of the gospel, 'Blessed are those…', are in the present tense. They are in the present tense because Jesus remains present in all believers through his Spirit, the Spirit of the risen Jesus. He said at the ascension, ' Know that I am with you always; yes, to the end of time' (Mt 28:20b).

CHAPTER THIRTEEN

The Road to Emmaus
(Luke 24:13-35)

There is only one thing certain in life and that is
that we will die some day. All of us fear death because
we fear the unknown. We only know life and even
Lazarus who was raised back to life (Jn 11:43-44)
eventually died again. Jesus did not return to life in
the way that Lazarus did; he returned to a life where
death has been overcome (1 Cor 15:26). This is why
the resurrection is so significant and we need to ask
the Holy Spirit to help us to enter into this mystery.

It is a mystery because life beyond death is outside our experience. During our lives, we have some
insight into what could be called 'little deaths' when
we experience losses such as tragedies, disappointments, betrayals – all these are negative experiences
and a kind of death. On the other hand, we also
experience 'little resurrections' such as celebrations,
births, marriages, successes – all positive experiences.
What we experience is a mixture of resurrections
and deaths but we do not understand what Jesus
meant when he said, 'I am the Life' (Jn 14:6). He

explained death in terms of life, (Jn 12:24-25). Essentially the passion demonstrated that the climax of a life of love is not death, a passing from this world to his Father, but the climax of a life of love is perfect love of God and neighbour (Mt 22:37-40). It is the final stage in the relationship which has been growing throughout our lives between us and God as our Father and between us and other people. As it says in the Preface for the Mass of the Dead, 'In death, life is not taken away, but only changed.' We must ask God our Father for the gift to understand that the goal of life is to be in him (Jn 17:24). This was Jesus' last petition on our behalf. This life, of course, is eternal life (Jn 17:3) and the reason for God the Father sending his Son (Jn 3:16) is to reveal what happens when one is faithful unto death, that at the end of this life, Easter heals Calvary.

The disciples cannot make sense of Jesus' recent death. Only the risen Jesus can help them understand the events of Good Friday and Easter Sunday. This is clearly shown in one of the most wonderful 'journey' stories ever told.

The journey to Emmaus takes place on Easter Sunday (v. 13). Who are the two disciples? Perhaps it is Cleopas (v. 18), and his wife Mary (Jn 18:25), who stood by the cross. They are some of his friends going through a crisis of faith (v. 21), which is exacerbated by the knowledge of what most of them had done. They had denied and deserted their closest friend Jesus just when he needed them most (Mk 14:50). They saw Jesus die and thought all was lost. Although the women, who found his tomb empty, declared he was alive (Lk 24:11). They feel sad, crushed by the death of their loving friend. They had 'heard' about the risen Jesus but had not seen him (Jn 20:29b). Cleopas and Mary cannot agree about what has happened. Joy has disappeared from their lives. Perhaps they are trying to forget by taking up their previous lives again (Jn 21:3), yet as they flee Jerusalem, the risen Jesus is pursuing them (v. 15). Just as once they followed him, he now follows them (Mk 10:21)!

The gospel states, 'Jesus came up and walked by their side.' He takes his pace from them; in other words, he joins them in their sorrow and, over the period of the journey gently leads them to recognise who he is. This takes a long time because he wants them to understand what they had experienced. Here, we see Jesus helping them to help themselves: helping them to clarify their thoughts and to realise what they are doing. His question to them seems brusque because they are brought up sharp, forced to forget their sorrow and answer the stranger's question (v. 17). He remains with them in their turmoil. Their answer is void because he is the only one who knows what has been happening! He does not say this however but gently continues to draw them out. They relate events as something that should not have happened, unaware that what happened was really good news. Jesus admonishes sharply, 'You foolish men!' because the good news should be proclaimed with joy (Lk 24:52). Joy is the essence of Christianity: 'Jesus is risen.' Sadness and gloom are barriers to the proclamation of the good news and so the Holy Spirit, who is joy itself, must be allowed to proclaim the word through them and through us (Jn 17:20). Perhaps we could examine ourselves and decide whether we ever proclaim the good news with joy. We must pray to achieve that joy of the Holy Spirit which Jesus had (Lk 10:21). To help them, Jesus starts by talking to them about what is familiar to them, about Moses and the prophets. He helps them realise that his death has changed, then in doing so he enables them to review their past differently. He helps them interpret the past in the light of what is now going on in their lives. What began as a chance encounter with a stranger, whom we do not like very much, can turn out to be the most important meeting of our lives. Here, the disciples are mourning not only the death of Jesus, but the death of their relationship with him. Jesus, in the disguise of a stranger, invites them to look back at their past again, despite their present sadness, but now with 'Easter' eyes. He gives a wholly different interpretation of the same event as he shows how his death, far from being a failure, is in fact the climax of his mission.

When we proclaim the good news, we need to remember that sacred scripture is the mind and the heart of God our Father; it will be different from our human way of thinking. God's plan, as partially outlined in scripture, is made clearer by other holy texts. This plan will be completed as he wills, rather than as we would like. Jesus' message is that for God the Father to accept suffering is to triumph (vv. 26-27, Is 50:51). The acceptance of the cross is not a catastrophe; it is a way of growing in love. 'It was necessary that the Christ should suffer and so enter into his glory' (v. 26). It will help us if we pray (Is 55:9-11):

'Yes, the heavens are as high above the earth, as my ways are above your ways, as my thoughts are above your thoughts. Yes, as the rain and the snow come down from the heavens and do not return without watering the earth, making it

yield and giving growth to provide seed for the
sower and bread for the eating, so the word that
goes from my mouth does not return to me
empty, without carrying out my will and suc-
ceeding in what it was sent to do'.

The Word will return to God our Father 'suc-
ceeding in what it was sent to do'. We should always
keep in mind what Jesus said to the Samaritan
woman, 'If you only knew what God is offering and
who it is that is saying to you ...' (Jn 4:10). God our
Father knows what is best for us and we must leave
it to him' (Lk 11:13).

When the risen Jesus explains scripture to them,
the meaning of life starts to become clear for the
disciples. Their spirits rise. As they draw near the
village, He offers to leave them, respecting their
freedom, but they press him to stay. What a tragedy
if they had let him go on! They invite Jesus in for a
meal and they 'break bread' together. In that instant,
their 'eyes are opened and they recognise him'. The
guest, who was invited to spend the evening with
them, becomes the host who feeds them. Perhaps
our prayer should be that of the blind man, 'Lord,
that I may see', or that God the Father 'may enlighten
the eyes of our mind', so that we, like the apostles,
recognise the presence of the risen Jesus (Eph 1:17-18).

The new relationship with the risen Jesus is now on a much deeper level. It has gone beyond merely seeing and touching (1 Jn 1:1), to hearing the word of God and celebrating the eucharist. Not only does Jesus help his disciples to interpret the past in their new experience of him as Lord, but he also gives them a new future. This new future is possible because their past has changed. They take the light of Easter Sunday back into the darkness of Good Friday and everything now looks different. Scripture does not tell us whether Jesus spoke, or put them on the right path, or was a good preacher. He just touches their hearts (v. 32). This experience enables them to set out at that instant to return to Jerusalem, which was a journey of about seven miles. They went out to tell their friends and to witness to the world the discovery they had just made, the experience of relationship that they had just undergone. It was because their hearts were burning that on listening to the risen Jesus 'they set out at that instant' and now his message flowed through them to others. As midday prayer of the Breviary says, 'and may that love within our hearts set fire to others with its flame'. We could use this as our own prayer. The Christian message is never fully complete until it is shared with others so that those who listen to our preaching can share in the same hope. On arrival, the disciples do not show any disappointment that they were not the first to discover that Jesus had risen (v. 34). On the contrary, they share the joy that Jesus appeared to all and that all can rejoice.

Perhaps what these two disciples experienced on their journey has been our experience. We may have been depressed because of broken relationships and sad events, wounded in some way or other in the past. This wonderful journey to Emmaus can help us to listen to the word of God and recognise him in the breaking of bread. This is the eucharist, which is celebrated each Sunday, commemorating the resurrection, which ends with: 'Let us go in peace and joy to love and serve the Lord.' Only then can we look with understanding at our past and, in hope, look to the future. 'Lord, I do believe, help the little faith that I have.'

CHAPTER FOURTEEN

Jesus appears to the apostles at Tiberias

Although St John's gospel finishes in Chapter 20. Chapter 21 was added by the early church. This account also illustrates the reality of the resurrection. It contradicts the allegations that the apostles merely had a vision or that what they saw was a figment of the imagination, or a ghost of the risen Jesus. It is unlikely that a vision or a spirit would point out a shoal of fish to a party of fishermen, or that a figment of the imagination would kindle a charcoal fire on the seashore, or that a ghost would cook a meal and share it out, yet, the risen Jesus does all things. How human he is in wanting all his friends to be 'at home' with him again!

Jesus' friends now get to 'know' in a way that changes their hearts and this, in turn, helps them see death in a different way (Lk 24:52). This new knowledge of Jesus (Jn 14:16-17) alters their whole perception. The evidence of the empty tomb could never, by itself, authenticate the resurrection. It is authenticated in this change of heart. We should continuously ask the Holy Spirit to give us the gift of Easter faith so that we too might experience a change of heart just as Jesus' friends did when he appeared to them and especially to Mary of Magdala and to Thomas, drawing away their hesitations.

Although she is talking to Jesus for some time, Mary does not recognise him (Jn 20:15b-16). She just sees a gardener (v. 15b). She is still fixed on the past and not aware of the present. Like Mary of Magdala, we must ask the Holy Spirit for the power to listen not just to the words but to the whole person. Very often, silence speaks louder than words. By spending time with Jesus, Mary of Magdala gets a deeper insight by her response, 'Rabbuni'.

Thomas first sees physical wounds. When he looks at Jesus, his eyes are opened, 'My Lord and my God' (Jn 20:27). The gospels do not say that he actually put his hand into the side of Jesus. Even if he had, it would not have been enough for him to see the divinity of Jesus.

We now have the culmination of all the experiences with Jesus, which began with Jesus challenging Andrew and John to 'come and see' (Jn 1:39). Now he invites them to 'come and have breakfast'. In prayerfully reflecting on this story, we are asking the Holy Spirit to help us know Jesus as a person, the

God-made-man, to enable each one of us to say, 'My Lord and my God' in our own unique way.

The disciples of Jesus return to work as fishermen as they do not know what else to do; they were still in shock after the events of the previous two or three weeks. There is, however, a distinct change in them. For example there is a new gentleness in Peter, 'I'm going fishing' and the others' response, 'We'll come with you' (v. 3). There is a new bond between them, created not just by the knowledge that they had let their friend down, but by the realisation that they all felt the same dejection, shame and hopelessness. It is then that Jesus reveals himself to them. While it is 'dark', not just because it is still night but because of the apparent absence of Jesus, these professional fishermen catch nothing (Lk 5:5). They never catch fish without Jesus' help in the gospels. As Jesus taught them: 'Cut off from me, you can do nothing' (Jn 15:5) When there is 'light', dawn, there too is Jesus, enlightening their minds (2 Pet 1:19b), 'dawn comes and the morning star rises in your minds'. Jesus' friends still do not recognise the stranger on the shore until Jesus reveals himself, when they listen to his command: 'Throw the net out to starboard and you will find something' (v. 6). There is an echo here of the Good Shepherd parable

(Jn 10:3-4). Because John is closely bound to Jesus in love, just as he was quick to understand when he saw the linen cloths lying on the ground in the empty tomb (Jn 20:8-9), he immediately says 'It is the Lord.' Each disciple only recognises the presence of Jesus in nature and things bit by bit, each in his own way. Jesus also reveals himself in ordinary domestic chores, as he builds a fire to cook breakfast for them (Mt 13:55). They recognise his presence by the abundance of fish, which recalls the abundance of loaves and fishes in the feeding of the 5,000 (Jn 6:12-13), and the huge quantity of water turned into wine at the wedding feast (Jn 2:6-9). Jesus would never be outdone in generosity.

Jesus is starting to teach his friends that he is present in everything in the world; he is not apart from the world. We need the Holy Spirit, the Spirit of the risen Jesus, to help us recognise his presence in all things and particularly in our neighbour. John, the beloved disciple, is led by the Holy Spirit to tell Peter, 'It is the Lord' (v. 7). Because of his closeness to Jesus, he has deeper insight and discernment. Here is an insight into the early church, where John passes on spiritual insight to someone in higher office (vv. 15-17, Lk. 22:32, 1 Pet 5: 7).

Peter is a very different man from John; he is a

man of action. This is how God the Father made him and he goes straight to Jesus leaving the others to bring the fishing boat, overloaded with fish, ashore. We see the risen Jesus still behaving like a servant preparing breakfast for the disciples, echoing the time (Jn 13:12-15) when Jesus washes his friends' feet. He still takes the initiative as he did in verse 4. He approaches them after their unsuccessful night fishing and tells them to cast their nets anew, to bring some of the fish ashore (v. 10). He turns their Christian sadness into joy, beyond their expectation. Jesus constantly comes to us through people and everyday events but, above all, he comes to us in prayer because he wants us to spend time with him.

Luke says that Peter obeyed Jesus and hauled the net to the shore. Luke uses the same word as is used by John, 'Draw', 'I shall draw all men to myself' (Jn 12:32). Jesus is now drawing people to himself, not just through his own ministry but also through Peter's and the apostles'. John is given the primacy of love and sensitivity in recognising Jesus, but Peter is first in the apostolic ministry. Peter takes the lead in hauling the net ashore. John seems to remember exactly how many fish were caught, 153. It is his way of saying that the church is wide enough to contain, within herself, all the peoples of the world. No one is excluded, not even the worst sinner.

This chapter was highly appropriate since fishing is an obvious metaphor for mission. Some interpret the failure to catch fish during the night as the unsuccessful preaching of the gospel to the Jews. They had more success when the risen Jesus told them to cast their nets elsewhere, namely among the non-Jews. This is when the converts started to stream in. St John is suggesting that the apostles should not be afraid to throw out their nets in uncharted waters (Mt 28:19-20). In addition, the reference to the net not being broken (v. 11b) has been interpreted to signify that the Christian community is not rent by schism, despite the huge numbers and different kinds of people brought into it. The unbroken net is, also, an indication of the abundance of Jesus' love to all who will trust him. It echoes the mission of the twelve (Mt 10).

'Come and have breakfast' (v. 12) recalls the time when the disciples had to come and see Jesus, discover him as a person (Jn 1:39). This knowledge of him is deepened now because it has a eucharistic dimension. In the feeding of the 5,000, Jesus gives thanks and the loaves and fishes are multiplied (Jn

6:11). This miracle occurred again on the shore of lake Tiberias. Just as St Luke in his account of the road to Emmaus (Lk 24:30) emphasises that the Emmaus disciples recognised Jesus in the breaking of bread, so 'Come and see' (Jn 1:39) is fulfilled at Tiberias (Jn 21:12). Their eyes are no longer blind. They are beginning to realise exactly who he is and they are in awe of him. They now know with the eyes of faith and love and so they use a divine title 'It is the Lord.' It is this knowledge that we are asking for. We really want to know Jesus the person, the God-made-man. We wish simply to say 'My Lord and My God'.

CHAPTER FIFTEEN

Jesus speaks to the apostles at Tiberias
(John 21:15-25)

Peter was among the group of disciples who made
the huge catch of fish. Fishing was always interpreted
in the early church as a symbol of mission, and the
promise of an abundance of converts is shown by
Jesus' command to throw the net to starboard, to
the unlikely part of the lake which speaks directly to
Simon. Jesus asks him an odd question, 'Simon, son
of John, do you love me more than these others do?'
(v. 15). Peter must have felt very embarrassed to have
this question asked, particularly in front of other
people. This suggests the question is very important
to Jesus. How human Jesus is, not frightened to
show his emotion! It is a very human of him to want
to be reassured of the love of somebody very close to
him. He may also be reminding Peter how at the last
supper he had boasted in front of all the other disciples how he was ready to die for him (Lk 22:31-34).
Now Jesus is talking to a very different Peter, a chast-
ened Peter, a Peter who has learnt humility through
his own weakness. Peter appeals to Jesus' knowledge
of what is in his heart, 'Lord, you know everything.'

John, unlike the synoptics, does not mention Jesus'
prediction of how Peter will disown. John has Jesus
question him three times about his love. Jesus realises
that Peter is a professional fisherman and so perhaps
his question also refers to all the material things
around them: the boat, the nets, the equipment, the
catch of fish. And he is asking Peter whether he is
willing to give them all up and devote his entire life
to Jesus and his mission. Again, Jesus is offering a
gift but it entails responsibilities (Jn 6:44). Now
Peter's love must spread to all people in order to
bring them back to the Father. That is why Peter
receives the authority of love, the sign of unity in
which everyone must be bound together. Jesus
shows more trust in Peter than Peter had in him. He
has to help Peter to realise that he is divine and to
understand that forgiveness is a divine act (Mk 2:7).
Peter realises that this knowledge is a gift from Jesus'
Father (Mt 16:17ff). Only when Peter realises how
much Jesus trusts him, can he accept the mission
entrusted to him.

Jesus tells Peter he is to be shepherd of his flock.
Peter knows the parable of the Good Shepherd (Jn
10), where Jesus proclaims that only he is the model
shepherd, the only way into the sheepfold (Jn 10:7).
He is the model shepherd because of the love he has
for his sheep (vv. 14-15). Anyone who is going to be

the shepherd of Jesus' flock must love Jesus in the same way that Jesus loves his father, (vv. 17-18). Jesus sends forth his friends as he was once sent by his Father (Jn 20:21). They are to participate in the same mission. Jesus, the model shepherd, makes Peter the shepherd tend his flock. These are the only shepherd images in the gospel. It is particularly significant that a reference to Peter's death immediately follows the command to tend the sheep (vv. 18-19). Among all the New Testament uses of shepherd imagery, only Jn 10 specifies that one of the duties of the model shepherd is to lay down his life for his sheep. In future, from now on, this must be the foundation in anyone holding pastoral office in the church. There is an important difference between Jesus and Peter. The flock will always belong to Jesus. 'They are … my lambs … my sheep.' They are never Peter's. Jesus' love for his sheep was never possessive. He regarded them as his Father's gift to him, (Jn 17:6), so the human shepherd must be reminded that the flock will always belong to Jesus, namely '… my lambs … my sheep'. No one can ever take the place of Jesus (Jn 10:14, 3-4). Maybe this is why Jesus addresses Peter as 'Simon, son of John' (v. 15), when he is receiving the role of shepherd, for the only other time Jesus calls him that is when he calls him the rock (Jn 1:42). Those in authority in the church and we, who are parents, will do well to pray the Good Shepherd parable in order to remind us that role of the good shepherd is to lead the sheep to pasture, (not take up the last position as in processions!), to know them one by one, and to lay down our lives for them. Maybe it is because he has to lead his flock and lay down his life in turn that Jesus warns Peter that, to be a good shepherd, he will inevitably be asked to lay down his life for his sheep (vv. 18-19). This he does years later in Rome, though he asks to be crucified upside-down since he is not worthy to be crucified like his Master. In this way, he was carrying out Jesus' last words to him, 'Follow me …' (vv. 19b, 22).

Although Jesus appoints Peter to be the leader of men, he also shows him (Jn 1:42) that, from the moment Jesus enters his life, he must be directed by him, instead of wanting to do everything by himself (Jn 21:18). This is a singular transformation by which we are all handed over to Jesus, and through which we glorify him. We glorify especially by the gift of self throughout our lives. We glorify him not by striving to do something extraordinary, but by recognising that we are limited in what we can achieve. It is enough that we simply try to be truly human. We can, for example, fast to provide money for the starving in under-developed countries; we

can try to live out our Christian values, treating one
another as unique human beings deserving of dignity,
seeing things from God the Father's point of view. It
is in this way that sometimes 'we must die daily' and
'go where we will not want to go'. Having understood that this is 'the way to give glory to God our
Father' (Jn 17:10b), each of us must listen to his
command, 'Follow me' and follow him in whatever
situation we find ourselves. It is when we suffer our
'little deaths' to self and selfishness that we are able
to love Jesus to the point of death (v. 19). Like Peter,
we are each just asked to return the love first given
to him (1 Jn 4:10-11). Like Peter, that is our calling,
the Christian calling and, in the end, it is the only
thing that matters.

Jesus' warning to Peter is addressed to us all (v. 18).
It is important that we grow old well. Growing old
is no joke. If only we could be like Bishop Helder
Camara and pray for the grace to grow old on the
outside without growing old on the inside, stay-
ing young, retaining hope, then we can still feel a
thousand reasons for living. Unfortunately, we take
the earth for granted. We trample on her throughout our lives and yet she continues to feed us. One
day, she will open up to receive us while we await the
resurrection. That grace of growing old well applies
just as much to St John (Jn 21:22-23). John's death of

old age was just as much a part of the Fathers' plan as Peter's. Both give glory to God the Father but in different ways. It was John's function to be pre-eminently the witness to Jesus, to be the witness of Love; Peter's role was to be the shepherd of Jesus, to go all over the world, shepherding his people as far as Rome. John lived on, probably at Ephesus, look-ing after Jesus' mother, Mary (Jn 19:27), contem-plating deeply Jesus' teaching until he was so old that he was past physical activity. At the end of John's gospel, Jesus is trying to tell Peter that we will each find fulfillment in whatever situation God the Father has placed us. There is no need for us to compare to others; our glory is in serving Jesus in whatever capacity has been allotted to us (v. 22). To be a disciple whom Jesus loves is, in the end, to be as close to him as someone who has been assigned church authority! If Peter has a primacy of pastoral care, John has another primacy bestowed by Jesus' love, namely, that of witness. The emphasis on love that John has in his first letter, especially at the end of his life (1 Jn 3: 14-19, 23; 4: 7-21), reminds us that Jesus was continually showing how much he cares. It is not the variety of gifts and destinies but the unity of love which in the end fulfills the Father's will. Ultimately, that is all that matters.

CHAPTER SIXTEEN

The Ascension
(Luke 24:50-53)

One of the happiest days of a student's life is graduation day. It is the culmination of years of study, a
time to say goodbye to teachers and staff, and the
first day of the rest of their lives. Usually, they are
encouraged to continue to study and deepen their
knowledge of their subject in order to progress in
their field of work. They will have to 'stand on their
own two feet' and rely on what they have already
learned from their teachers.

In a certain sense the ascension experience, or
the last appearance of the risen Jesus to his friends,
is like a graduation ceremony. Jesus had been
instructing his disciples, men and women, throughout his life, not only in public (Mt 13:24) but in
private (Jn 13:36). Up until now, they were 'disciples',
that is students, but now he makes his 'apostles' his
ambassadors (2 Cor 5:20). From now on they will be
on their own. They will no longer be able to come
back to their Master to share their experiences (Lk
10:17) and their joy (v. 21). Jesus tells them, however,

that they will not be entirely alone. They will have the help of the Spirit (Lk 24:49). In this way, therefore, they will remain his disciples, always be deepening their understanding of Jesus' teaching (Jn 14:26).

What is happening in this ascension experience? Jesus is really returning to his Father (Acts 1:9-11). He has completed his mission and his Father is taking him home. It is a most intimate meeting: 'Well done thou good and faithful servant … enter into the joy of the Lord.' The Father joyfully greets his Son, who is now fully permeated by the Holy Spirit. In our prayer we can ask that we might enter the atmosphere of the ascension. We should try and be joyful for them. We need to be filled with reverence and awe at what is taking place.

Like any other human being before he departs, Jesus wants to mark his departure in a special way. Besides a meal, he does it by transforming, through his Holy Spirit, these men and women. Having been reconciled to him, they are joyful that they can pass on this reconciliation. All jealousy has gone, there is no more arguing about procedure (Mk 9:34). The Holy Spirit is gradually influencing them more and more.

It was essential they should experience the ascension because something had to happen. It was unthinkable that the appearances of the risen Jesus should become fewer and fewer, simply finally petering out. That would effectively have wrecked the faith of the disciples. The ascension is, of course, described in Jewish terms, but there had to come in some way or another an 'hour' when the Jesus of earth became the Christ of heaven. The ascension meant a number of things to the disciples. By praying it, it becomes meaningful for us all. It marked an ending. One stage was past – the first stage of their friendship. They had shown faith in a flesh and blood human being like themselves. His physical presence was linked to time and space. Now his presence became independent of time and space. The ascension was also a new beginning. Although they left him for the last time, they didn't leave the mountain broken hearted, they left him with great joy (Lk 24:52). They were not being stoic, it was simply that that they knew that they had a master from whom nothing can separate them, not even betrayal, or death (Rom 8:38-39). To sustain them, they had a constant awareness that they had a friend interceding before God the Father for them (Heb 7:25), One whom they had loved on earth. They knew their prayer would be taken up in their friend's intercessory prayer before his Father. Their prayer was Jewish, like Jesus', and so they returned in joy to the temple to praise God. They are starting their journey back to their Father in the same atmosphere, peace and joy, as the gospel began, although it is now Christianised. St. Mathew puts it another way: at the conception, Joseph is told Jesus' name will be 'Emmanuel' that is, God-with-us (Mt 1:23), and this is confirmed by Jesus on the mountainside in Galilee at the ascension (Mt 28:20), when he tells his friends, 'I am with you always to the end of time.' The gospel tells us how the human expression of God the Father, Jesus, did this and actually fulfilled himself and enabled us to become his brothers and sisters (Jn 20:17b). Perhaps it due to that that there doesn't seem to be any nostalgia for the 'good old days' with Jesus during his mortal life, which is really quite remarkable.

Jesus' actions, words and life are now being understood in the light of Easter faith. As his disciples, we are encouraged to look forward to his Second Coming, the *Parousia,* (see Chapter 19), when everything will become clear and the Father's plan is completed. To do this, and it applies to us as well, there are the 'powers' that the risen Jesus gave his disciples. These are demonstrated in the different atmospheres prevailing in the past few weeks during the passion. Then the sheep were scattered; now they are united; then there was sorrow and anguish; now there is peace and joy. Then God the Father seemed absent; now he is present through his Spirit. Death clothed the air; now life prevails. This is the atmosphere imbuing the disciples. Basically it changed the quality of their lives, allowing the faith, trust and confidence that the risen Jesus has for these men and women, and can do the same for us today. They needed this and we do, too, if we are going to bring the good news to others in this secular and cynical society. What chance had his disciples? Look at those men: ignorant Jewish fishermen being sent out into a world, as anti-Semitic as it is today, to preach about a crucified Galilean carpenter, a message which with their religious background would have been 'heretical'. He never wrote a book, never went beyond the boundaries of Palestine. He preached a message which was laughed at by the intelligent Greek world (Acts 17:32), dismissed by the power of Rome and attacked by the religion of Judaism. These men and women return to the Temple (Lk 24:52-53), praising the Lord Jesus in the full sight of the High Priest and Sanhedrin. They must have been confused, especially to see Peter who they knew had denied Jesus publicly more than any of the others. Now he seems to be the leader and preaching that his Master was the Son of God in the divine sense! It was all topsy-turvy. This small band of insignificant men and women were all aware of this incongruity, no doubt fearful and hesitant, yet despite all that, they knew that Jesus, through his Spirit, was working through them, (Mt 10:20). If we can appreciate that Jesus works through us too, then the peace of Christ, not the world's peace (Jn 14:27), will be the quality of our calling.

In one sense, the ascension is, to put it simply, a summons to work. This perhaps is borne out by the fact that it is always celebrated, rather unusually, on a Thursday. This is because the ascension is celebrated exactly forty days after Easter. Thursday is part of the working week. This helps us to understand that there is no real distinction between ordinary time and religious, sacred time, and that God is as much present in the workplace as in a church or monastery. Jesus himself said, 'I am with you always, even to the end of time.' So Jesus is present in our time as well as in eternity. Jesus is always present, that is why God's name, Yahweh, is so important. In Hebrew, Yahweh means 'I am, who am'. It does not mean 'I was … or I will be …' He is 'I am', always in the present. We would all greatly benefit from trying to live more in the present, because most of us either worry or are preoccupied about the past or the future, finding it difficult to live in the 'here and now'. God is there.

The angels chastised Jesus' friends for lingering to watch Jesus' ascension (Acts 1:11). According to St Luke, the angels told them to go back to their normal work and rhythm of life and wait for the coming of the Holy Spirit. The risen Jesus had told them to go and baptise in his name and 'make disciples of all the nations' (Mt 28:20). He needed their unique personalities, their whole beings to bring the good news of his Father to everyone in a way that he could not. Although he was God he was also a human being, limited like all of us, but he now knows us from the inside, what it is to be a human being, because of all his own human experiences (Heb 2:16-18).

Jesus wanted them to preach and teach (Acts 2:14, 38-41). This militates against our secular society that wants religion to be a private matter and holds that it is wrong to promote faith and Christianity. Even Christians can get embarrassed about talking about their faith – even with fellow Christians. All of us breathe in the secular atmosphere and so it is important that we pray for the courage to speak out when necessary (Acts 5:29, 40-42). To tell the truth against all the odds, friendship with Jesus can blossom in human lives (Eph 3:20). His message is one of love, love for everybody, since each individual is a unique image of his Father, and he needs his friends to allow his love to flow through them to all and sundry. Love is catching. We could use the midday prayer of the church in trying to pray the ascension experience. It sums up this work of evangelisation:

> May mind and tongue, made strong in love,
> Your praise throughout the world proclaim,
> And may that love within our hearts,
> Set fire to others with its flame.

CHAPTER SEVENTEEN

To be an apostle of the risen Jesus
(Matthew: 18-20; Luke: 24:45-48)

We have to listen to this command to go forth and teach all nations (Mt 20:18-20). We know we are very inadequate for this work, but we are encouraged by the knowledge that the risen Jesus is always with us. 'Emmanuel', God with us, is both at the beginning (Mt 1:23), and at the end of the gospel. It shows us how Jesus, the human expression of God the Father, actually fulfilled himself in human life and so enables us to become his brothers and sisters (Jn 20:17), his disciples of today. In this experience we need the Holy Spirit of the risen Jesus working through us, so that we really learn who he is and are constantly sustained, strengthened and renewed. This is how we shall be gradually making the resurrection experience our own. This is important because the risen Jesus is sending us out as apostles of the resurrection.

What makes an apostle? An apostle is somebody who is sent to be spent. He is sent above all to give himself as Jesus did (Jn 20:21). An apostle therefore is not somebody sent to do a job and then report back but someone who is taken up in generating more and more love, which is the life of the triune God. It is the ministry of 'infecting' people with love, namely spreading the work of causing love universally (Mt 5:44-48). This is a challenging ministry for it calls us to see the truth about ourselves and our society – no easy task in the Western world of constant entertainment, anaesthetised conscience (where no one takes personal responsibility) and hidden injustice. It requires us to walk with our heads in heaven (Heb 7:25) so that we can avoid being reduced to people with no hope or interest beyond this world. It requires us, however, to walk with our feet on earth (Acts 1:11): work has to be done and the gospel preached. It is a balance of both, for Jesus did not come to inaugurate a 'kingdom of this world' (Jn 18:36), although he was tempted to do so, (Mt 4:9), and by an enthusiastic crowd (Jn 6:15). Despite our call to be 'in the world', our final home is heaven (Eph 2:19, Heb 11:13).

We pay a price of being an apostle. We are trying to show forth the love of Jesus by which we are consumed. There is an extra dimension to this love, namely redemptive love (1 Jn 4:10). This dimension will be inevitable because any apostle will experience the pain of the world's lack of love for God. God as Father, and particularly as Father, is vulnerable to his children's response to his love, just as Jesus, his Son, was vulnerable to the response of his brothers and sisters (Lk 23:34). The Spirit of both is vulnerable to the cruelty and insensitivity of people to one another (1 Jn 3:16-17). This cruelty comes from the love of power, selfishness, possessiveness.

Being asked to be an apostle to witness to the risen Jesus might make us worry about the quality of our lives, about what other people might expect from us or might see in us. Unless the Spirit of God is allowed to dominate, we, his apostles, can easily become self-centred and self pre-occupied. Paul puts it very well when he emphasises that it is primarily God the Father at work, the work reconciling first of all the apostle himself (2 Cor 5:18-20). Unless we experience reconciliation we cannot pass it on to others (2 Cor 1:3-4). We apostles are to be the ambassadors of Jesus, that is we are to convey to others how Jesus thinks and lives. As ambassadors, we 're-present' Jesus to others. Paul goes on to tell us that God the Father appeals through us. In some mysterious way, God the Father needs our unique personalities to bring over the good news of reconciliation to others, otherwise his plan will be thwarted both within ourselves and in others.

In addition, according to Peter, an apostle is somebody who must spend time with the risen Jesus (Acts 1:21-22), namely, the time from Jesus' baptism until his ascension. Spending time is essential when you want to know a person deeply. It is by spending time with someone that you obtain intuitive knowledge of that person. You can always read about somebody, or listen to others speaking about a person, but until you meet and spend time with someone, you do not really know that person. To spend time with Jesus, the Son of God, is of the utmost importance, because this is how he shares with us his own personal experience of his Father's love for him, and also his love for his Father and his fellow human beings. Just like all friendship, it will be a two way process. We will be required to commit our whole self to Jesus, continually relying on his word and trusting him. We will be required to be receptive, being gradually more and more enlightened as we contemplate and listen to his word, and gain knowledge. This is shown when Jesus takes the initiative asking, 'What do you want?' (Jn 1:38) The response is 'Rabbi, where do you live?' He challenges them to 'come and see'. It is by coming to him, spending time with him, talking to him, getting to know him, that they become good friends. This is commitment. It is the normal human experience of friendship. Enlightenment comes from the intuitive knowledge of him as a person. This is demonstrated when Andrew tells his brother, Simon Peter, 'We have found the Messiah' (v. 41), not just that he has found a Rabbi. He has deeper knowledge; he has discovered the Messiah. It is by coming and spending time with the risen Jesus that we, too, receive the revelation of the Father, the experience of his love. After Jesus met Philip and commanded him, 'Follow me' (Jn 1:43), Philip managed to persuade Nathaniel, despite his prejudice, to come and see too (v. 46) and both of them returned to Jesus to behold him more. One can never fully plumb the depths of a person, and how much more so if that person is divine. Nevertheless, their superficial view of him as Rabbi or Messiah, becomes much deeper when they see him as Lord, Son of the Father, and ultimately as 'My Lord and my God', which should be our prayer as well.

Perhaps the whole focus of a disciple's life should be to try and enter into that command of love, 'come and see', and to follow the lead of the Holy Spirit in bringing that knowledge to others by saying 'We have seen the Lord' (Jn 20:18-25). One process reinforces the other. The more I enter into 'come and see' and bring that knowledge over to others and the more knowledge I have of the Lord, the more I want to 'come and see'. In this way, I am open to his light and surrender to the action of the Holy Spirit (2 Cor 3:18). In consequence, my new witness to him has a deeper ring of sincerity, a more persuasive tone of conviction. 'If we knew how to look at life through God the Father's eyes, all life would be a sign. If we only knew how to listen to God, all life would be a prayer' (M. Quoist). If I do not follow his 'come and see', I become 'simply a gong booming, or a symbol clashing'. This metaphor describes even the best intentioned Christian activity if it is not the fruit of waiting upon God with prayer and silence, attentively listening to discover his purpose. It is not enough simply to listen to ourselves, to our own ideas, to act according to what we think that purpose should be. Part of all this power is to submit, gradually, the whole of ourselves to the rhythm of the Spirit of the risen Jesus. It is also to discover his Father's purpose, and the fruit of all this listening and witnessing will be to bring that same Spirit to others. We saw, earlier, how Jesus told Mary of Magdala that she no longer needs to hold on to his bodily presence. She has seen beyond outward appearances and can grasp him as the Divine

Person, the Eternal Son and, by faith and love, through the Holy Spirit, she can hold him permanently in her heart. Our mission is to go and tell others, to bear witness of this (Jn 20:17), and to bring others to Jesus, that he may bring them to his Father.

Only those, like the apostles, who know him in this way, can be sent to tell others because it is as ourselves, and through the relationships we make with other people, that we can reach out to others (Jn 20:19-20). Only when the apostles had seen him as Lord, did Jesus say, 'As the Father sent me, so am I sending you.' 'Receive the Holy Spirit. For those whose sins you forgive, they are forgiven; and for those whose sins you retain, they are retained' (Jn 20:21-23). Only then, they who had first found the risen Jesus, can tell others where to find him. 'We have seen the Lord' (v. 25). Only then can they make 'disciples of all nations' (Mt 28:19). They do this by mingling authority and compassion, both of which they had already received in their own lives (Mt 7:29, Jn 8:11). Only prayer can help them and us, today's disciples, to mingle authority and compassion into a Christ-like way of teaching. The Holy Spirit did it initially through the first disciples (Jn 20:22), and also will do it through others, as long as the good news will be spread (Jn 17:20). In this way, the Holy Spirit will help all disciples down the ages to 'teach them to observe all the commandments I have given' (Mt 28:18-20). The risen Jesus wants his disciples of all generations to teach his commandments. Moses' commandments have been superseded. St John tells us that we are to live the life God the Father wants. We are to commit ourselves to his Son Jesus and to love one another as he told us to (Jn 15:12). Because he has given us the Holy Spirit, we can accomplish these commandments and help others to do the same. They are above all, commandments about how to conduct personal relationships. And to help us succeed we could well reflect on the promises made to Ezekiel (Ezek 36:26-27) and pray for the same grace:

> I shall give you a new heart and put a new spirit in you;
> I shall remove the heart of stone from your bodies
> And give you a heart of flesh instead.

CHAPTER EIGHTEEN

Pentecost: Sending the Holy Spirit

Jesus only mentions the Holy Spirit when he is going away. It is only in the context of Jesus leaving that we begin to understand who the Holy Spirit is. As long as he is physically present, Jesus is confined in time and space; he can only reach the people he actually meets. Through Jesus' disciples, the Holy Spirit will be able to reach everyone, wherever and whenever they live. The apostles were sad at the coming departure of Jesus (Jn 16:12-13). They felt they were being robbed of Jesus because the world had judged and condemned him. Jesus had warned them about this, that the world would rejoice when they were sad, and it is at this moment that he offers them consolation, promising that he will send them the Holy Spirit. It is important to realise that it is to the advantage of the apostles that Jesus goes, because otherwise the Holy Spirit cannot come to them (Jn 16:7-8).

Jesus sends his Holy Spirit at Pentecost for two reasons. Firstly so that the Holy Spirit will deepen their knowledge of who Jesus is; and, secondly, so that the Holy Spirit will enlighten their minds about how he thought and how he loved. In this way, he enkindles their love for Jesus (Jn 14:26).

In the Old Testament, the Spirit of God hovers over the waters. It is the Spirit of the Father and the Son and is revealed as a divine force (Gen 1:2). Later on, this divine force transforms human beings and makes them capable of performing exceptional deeds: like Saul (1 Sam 11:6) and David (1 Sam 17:50-51); or of prophesying like Jeremiah (Jer 1:6 9), and Isaiah (Is 6:5-9, Ezek 37); or of performing a particular mission, like Mary (Lk 1:35). To these the Spirit brings a special understanding of God (Is 55:8-11). The Spirit does not remain with them, however. We are told, 'There was no Spirit as yet, because Jesus had not yet been glorified' (Jn 7:39). As yet, the Spirit is not the Spirit of God-made-Man and so she has to remain remote. Though each sending of the Spirit is deeper than before, she remains fluid and infiltrates imperceptibly, remaining invisible.

The Holy Spirit does not need to have the same impact on Jesus because right from his conception, the Spirit dwells in him. She even brought about his very existence (Mt 1:20; Lk 1:35). The Holy Spirit is on him (Lk 4:18), his very existence is holy. He is in the Holy Spirit and the Holy Spirit is in him (Jn 16:13-14).

The Spirit is 'restricted' by the normal limits of Jesus' individuality and his sphere of activity as a human being, as long as he remains on earth. When Jesus dies, he gives up his Spirit (Jn 19:30), so that at Pentecost, it is not just God, Father and Son, who sends his Spirit as he does in the Old Testament, but it is God and the risen Jesus who now send the Spirit (Lk 24:49). It is a much deeper sending than before, because it is not just God who sends, as in the Old Testament, but also the risen Jesus. In other words, the Holy Spirit is sent by both God and man now. It is a deeper sending because the Holy Spirit is no longer restricted. She is sent to create the infant church (Acts 2:1-4) and needs to be able to influence the whole world (Mt 28:18-20; Lk 24:44-49). She now resides permanently in the church and will never be taken away from her (Mt 28:20). Only the Spirit of the Risen Christ understands that Christ is divine, the human expression of the Father. Only the Spirit of God-made-Man makes it possible for anyone to live with the risen Christ (1 Jn 1:1-4), to know and love him as he really is – divine, but human like us (Phil 3:7-10). He is no longer remote but able to identify totally with man in his human condition (Heb 2:16-18). Because we have been given this gift Jesus said to the crowds, 'I tell you solemnly, of all the children born of women, a greater than John the Baptist has never been seen; yet the least in the kingdom of heaven is greater than he is' (Mt 11:11)

In the first place, the Holy Spirit will show men that they had the wrong idea of sin. When the Jews crucified Jesus, they believed they were serving God, but when the story of the crucifixion was later preached, they were 'cut to the heart' (Acts 2:37). They realised not only that they had sinned, but the enormity of their sin. Who gives this insight to them? It is the Holy Spirit. Pilate declared Jesus to be innocent three times (Jn 18:38; 19:4, 6), but he was faced with a stubborn refusal to believe in Jesus. Preferring darkness to light (Jn 3:19), this stubborn refusal to believe is their sin. This is illustrated clearly in Jn 9 where a man born blind is cured. The Pharisees start off with an open mind as they enquire about the cure (v. 15). They then begin to rationalise (v. 18). Their attitude hardens (v. 24). Then they abuse the man (v. 29), and finally drive him away (v. 34). They make their blindness permanent (vv. 40-41). We need to understand that the guilty are not just those who crucified Christ. They are those of every generation who are hostile to him. Our lack of belief expresses itself today in the way we are so caught up with materialism, substituting possessions for God. The Holy Spirit comes, therefore, to show us that our fundamental sin is not to let Jesus into our hearts, that there is still 'no room at the inn'.

Secondly, the Holy Spirit will show us that the world was wrong about who 'was right'. The 'Jews' regarded Jesus' claim to be one with the Father (Jn 5:18) as blasphemous. The purpose of the trial was to show that he was not the Son of God (Jn 19:7), but the Holy Spirit has again worked a reversal of the world's judgement. Jesus was given a punishment that the worst criminals had to suffer, and branded as an enemy of God. Nevertheless, there were people who recognised the Son of God in this crucified figure. To them, this terrible death sentence showed that Jesus was precisely what he claimed to be. This is how the centurion recognised Jesus as the Son of God (Mt 27:54). The Holy Spirit is sent to us so that in the rejects of society, in their vulnerability, we recognise the Son of God. The Holy Spirit helps Paul see Jesus on the road to Damascus (Acts 9:1-9) This Holy Spirit enables people put their trust for all eternity in this crucified Jewish criminal. The Spirit convinces us that Jesus is victorious over death. The Holy Spirit is meaningless and self-contradictory if Jesus has not overcome death. After twenty centuries, people are still willing to live their lives for him. He died a despicable death but they believe he is still alive today. People wouldn't give themselves like this to a dead hero.

Thirdly, the Holy Spirit will show us that the world was wrong 'about judgement'. 'Are you the Son of God?' is the perennial question. It is asked by leaders (Lk 23:35), by the soldiers (v. 37), by one of the thieves (v. 39). The world thinks that if he is the Son of God, he should come down from the cross. But it is precisely because he stays on the cross that Jesus proves he is God. Love, ultimately forgiving love, conquers all people (v. 34), and gathers them into a unity (Jn 11:51-52). The people who were judging Jesus, who decided he was not the Son of God because he stayed nailed to the cross, were judging themselves. It was they who failed to understand that love can conquer hearts. However powerful a king might be, whatever he might impose on a conquered people, he cannot conquer a person's heart. It's because of Jesus' love that Satan loses his grip and that evil is overcome. No wonder the chief priests and pharisees said, 'This is only the beginning' (Mt 27:64; 28:15). The Holy Spirit gives us insight into God's judgements.

At Pentecost, we have three groups of people in one room awaiting the coming of the Holy Spirit that Jesus had promised (Jn 16:7). These groups consist of Mary and Jesus' relatives, the eleven disciples and the women of Galilee. These make up the basic community of the church. Together they witness to the beginning of Jesus' life right through to the beginning of the life of the church. Mary and Jesus' relatives bear witness to the beginnings of Jesus' life, as described in the infancy narratives; the eleven apostles witness the mortal life of Jesus and the women of Galilee witness the resurrection appearances of Jesus at the beginning of 'Eastertide'. All bear witness to the gospel and await the coming of the Holy Spirit in prayer. Like Mary at the incarnation (Lk 1:26ff), they await the Word of God to shape their lives. They have the conviction that this is where it will happen and they wait together. The Jews celebrated the feast of Pentecost on the fiftieth day after the Exodus. It was on this day that God renewed his covenant with his people through the power of the Holy Spirit. It was at Pentecost that all those people from the far flung reaches of the Roman Empire converged on Jerusalem (Acts 2:8-11). It was time for a new beginning, a new creation. Through the Holy Spirit a whole new life was possible.

Jesus had told Nicodemus (Jn 3:3-8), that the Holy Spirit would be known through her activities. She is like a gust of wind. We do not notice the wind directly, but we know when it is present because we hear the leaves rustle and see the branches sway. This is how the presence of the Holy Spirit is discerned (Acts 2:1-4), this happening 'like a powerful wind from heaven', when 'something appeared to them that seemed like tongues of fire'. In Hebrew, the same word 'rhuah' is used for both 'spirit' and 'breath'. Both are so important for the mission of the church since both are connected with communication. When we converse with one another, we form relationships with one another, we bring life to one another. Breath carries our words and, in this way, we are a channel of the Holy Spirit to one another (Mt 10:20). Again, the second symbol of the Holy Spirit, fire, constantly appears when we talk of relationships between people. For example, when we smile and say 'hello', people 'warm' to us, their eyes light up, a warm personality is responsive. The opposite is also true, for example we can 'cut a person dead' or 'freeze somebody out' (Eph 4:29-30).

The Holy Spirit can be seen in all relationships; in loving parents, in caring friends who stand by us come what may, in the stranger who takes the first step of friendship, there is the Spirit of God. In relationships which remain faithful and lasting and life giving, the Spirit of God heals, warms and reconciles. The Spirit of God is at home in us (Rom 8:15), and in the Spirit we are related to others (Rom 8:16). By our relationships we know that God is in us and we are in God (1 Jn 4:13). Just as it is by the effects of the wind on the trees that we know that there is a wind at all, so it is in our relationships that we know God is within us and we are in God.

We see another aspect of the warmth of the Holy Spirit when we are told that people are bewildered yet delighted on hearing the apostles speak their own languages (Acts 2:5-7): 'Now you are speaking my language.' When this happens, people warm to us, we become united. When they hear this language of the Holy Spirit, they learn too the language of forgiveness, love and understanding. The language of the Holy Spirit, the language of love, becomes the universal tongue, the most profound language and it is through this that first Peter (v. 14ff), then the apostles, learn to reach out to all people. This language of the Holy Spirit finally overcomes the ancient division of men's tongues that began at Babel (Gen 11:5-9).

Loneliness is just as prevalent today as was when Adam and Eve sewed together fig leaves to make their clothes. Too many people still feel cut off, out of touch, still suffer the confusion of Babel and suffer the dramatic loneliness of Job (Job 19:13-22). Yet Pentecost shows that God the Father has created us all to be in relationships and in this way to spread the good news: that he is the Father, that we are all, along with the risen Jesus, his sons and daughters and that all human beings are brothers and sisters of one another. It is the Spirit who makes us all one family in the image of the family of God, Father, Son and Holy Spirit (Gen 1:26).

CHAPTER NINETEEN

Come Lord Jesus

Immediately after the consecration at Mass we say: 'Christ has died, Christ is risen, Christ will come again.' At the very moment of his sacramental presence, we are ready to greet him when he comes again in glory. He is here but he is not here. During the Mass, especially in the Creed, we pray of his death, his resurrection and his coming in glory. We have to try and experience in some way these three stages of his life. We need to rejoice at his presence, constantly aware of his sacrifice and look forward to his second coming. In the early church, this second coming was thought to be imminent and Christians were expected to be ready. Since the early church believed that the *Parousia* was imminent, so there was a feeling that there was no need for permanence and stability. A community of love would suffice until Jesus returned. As time went on, the church started to recognise that her mission was not to be accomplished so quickly and so its apostolic form of simplicity of doctrine, practice and authority was inadequate. The work of the Holy Spirit however would endow it with the inner strength to overcome the erosion of time and cultural changes. The church, therefore, acquired a more rigid structure but unfortunately in consequence the church gradually lost the feeling that 'Christ will come again', although in theory she had not abandoned her teaching on it. Perhaps this is why it does not seem to loom large in our prayer during the Advent season, yet it is an important tributary to our personal and communal prayer.

Both in the New Testament and in ordinary life, there is a great deal about the 'end times', so to help us into the atmosphere of looking forward to Jesus' return, one of Jesus' parables, which is constantly used in the church's liturgy, could be read (Mt 25:1-13). In many of his parables, Jesus compares the kingdom of God to a wedding. Why? A Jewish wedding is a great and joyous occasion, involving the whole Jewish community. 'Everyone from six to sixty will follow the marriage drum' is a Jewish saying. Usually the bride awaits the arrival of the bridegroom at her own home. Her friends, acting as bridesmaids, meet the groom when he comes with his friends, then help to escort the couple back to his home, where the wedding feast will be celebrated. In the parable, the bridegroom is late – unlike ours when it is usually the bride! But when he does arrive five bridesmaids are ready to greet him and accompany him to his house. The other five are not prepared.

Traditionally, the couple does not go away on honeymoon but stay in their home for a week for the most important celebration of their lives. Their close friends were invited to these festivities and so these five bridesmaids missed not only the marriage ceremony, but also the week of celebration because they were unprepared.

Those hearing Jesus' parable would have been used to having the relationship between God and his people expressed in terms of the bride and bridegroom. The Covenant is seen in terms of a marriage. The bridegroom is God and the Chosen People the bride. They would not have understood the individual as the bride of God because, for them, the bride was always the people as a whole. In the parable, Jesus is warning them to be prepared, to watch, not to be like the ten bridesmaids who dozed! When the Messiah came, many people were like the five foolish bridesmaids, unprepared and therefore blind to his presence in their midst. He warns them to have the right relationship with God because they cannot suddenly create a relationship when he does come.

They must possess it already. In the parable, the lack of oil signified lack of relationship, a sign of unwillingness.

The wisdom of the other five bridesmaids consisted in doing what was expected of them, in being prepared for the arrival of the bridegroom. Their wisdom wasn't extraordinary, so much as eminently practical. Their wisdom consisted merely in having flasks of oil to go with their lamps. Meister Eckhart, a mystic of the fourteenth century, summed it up perfectly when he said 'Wisdom consists in doing the next thing you have to do, doing it with your whole heart and finding delight in doing it.'

Jesus shows in much of his preaching how important it is to be prepared, to be like the wise bridesmaids. It took quite a while for his words to penetrate as is illustrated in the following examples (Mk 4:1ff). It takes time for Mary of Magdala to understand that she has found Jesus again (Jn 20:16-17); for Peter to weep and return to Jesus (Lk 22:62 and Jn 21:17); for the Emmaus pilgrims to recognise him (Lk 24:31); for Thomas and the apostles to believe (Jn 20:27-28).

Again, when he told Thomas that he was 'the Way, the Truth and the Life', he showed himself as one of the 'wise bridesmaids'. Here, in ordinary life, we have wisdom, for we all wait to be born and for this to happen every human being has to wait in darkness. Once darkness is touched by light, the darkness goes and light dawns unfailingly (Jn 1:5), just as day dawns after the night. As the baby grows towards the light, there is a certain aloneness (Ps 139:13-15), although he is awaited in hope especially by God his Father and those who love him. For a while nothing seems to be happening, yet the greatest of all happenings is taking place. It is a time for waiting. Perhaps this is occurring in us now (2 Cor 3:18), for all mortal lives are really going towards the time of light (Jn 9:5), 'I am the light of the world' and are all finally tumbled into the light of God Our Father's presence at death (Eph 1:4b).

There is another way of looking at it – being prepared and not prepared – five like the bridesmaids were ready and five were not – is similar to what is meant by 'judgement' in St John's gospel. The coming referred to here was the incarnation (Jn 1:14). When he comes, people react differently, some listen and believe (Jn 1:12-13), some refuse and won't believe (v. 11). There are two examples (Mt 2: 1-12), the visit of the magi or astrologers; and Jesus' trial before Pilate (Jn 18:33 -19:16).

In the first example, the magi or astrologers sought God in the stars and so God spoke to them through a star. The astrologers followed the star across the desert out of devotion to truth. They were committed to truth from the moment they set out, before they even knew the name of Jesus. By the time they reached Herod's court, they were not vaguely seeking enlightenment, ready to revere whatever was true and good. They were much more definite than that, 'Where is the newborn King of the Jews? We have come to worship him.' They were prepared to believe in whatever reality their star was leading them to and they discovered the reality of Jesus. Their search for truth was a free choice that involved risk. They had to decide whether or not to accept the evidence that was coming to them from within. If the star was a sign from God and they did not follow it, they would miss the most important and fulfilling meeting of their lives. On the other hand to follow a star out into the desert just on the off chance that it might be a sign from God, seemed a lack of common sense. They did not know how far would it lead them, how long they would be gone, or even whether they would ever return. They just had to respond and find out for themselves (Mt 14:28-29).

The other example of a free choice being made concerns Pilate. Before Pilate, the pharisees indict

Jesus as a criminal. Pilate has a choice. He can release Jesus or he can crucify him but he wants a compromise. He wants to save Jesus whom he recognises as innocent and yet he also wants to save his reputation in Rome. Pilate is trained and skilled in compromise and searches for a third choice. But, before Jesus, there can be no compromise; Pilate has either to accept or reject Jesus. Twice he asks Jesus about his kingdom (Jn 18:33), and Jesus gives Pilate an insight into his kingdom (Jn 18:37), when he speaks of truth and witness and offers him the choice of accepting his kingdom or rejecting it. By these means Jesus also warns his friends what choice for him implies (Jn 15:18-20). Pilate tries to transfer the accountability to others, but each person has to choose Jesus for himself (Mt 27:24-25). What a low game Pilate plays and what a high price Jesus has to pay! This is the price of compromise.

We all compromise. On the day at our marriage or ordination we say we will give everything, but gradually, bit by bit, we renege. We put up limits on what we are prepared to give. Let us pray that we never hear '… you have less love for me now than you used to have' (Rev 2:3-4). A disciple is one who accepts the wisdom of God the Father (Jn 6:66-68), who wants and values knowledge of him and whom wisdom 'instructs' through Jesus (Lk 9:35). God our Father gives himself by revelation and we can either say 'yes' or 'no' to that revelation. But the second coming will embrace everyone. It will be universal. Jesus gives us the ability to be awake, to listen and believe. He is at work in each one of us so that we are ready to receive the summons of his Father (Jn 14:3), ready to be reunited with our best friend. This expectation should colour the whole of our outlook (1 Thess 5:1-11). This is the way we should be with Jesus, otherwise our prayer 'Come, Lord Jesus' will not be a real longing in us. This hope of seeing him again must colour the whole of our lives and therefore the whole of our prayer, so that this longing will come over to others and help them to see the fulfilment of the Father's plan in Jesus, in him who is the 'Alpha and the Omega, the Beginning and the End' (Rev 21:6a).